Whole
Body Reset Diet

1500 Days' Delicious Recipes Using Minimally Processed Foods, and a 4-Week Meal Plan to Boost Metabolism and Achieve a Flat Belly & Optimal Health in Your Midlife and Beyond

Lucia Johnson

© Copyright 2022 – All rights reserved.

The content contained within this book may not be reproduced, duplicated or transmitted without direct written permission from the author or the publisher.
Under no circumstances will any blame or legal responsibility be held against the publisher, or author, for any damages, reparation, or monetary loss due to the information contained within this book, either directly or indirectly.

Legal Notice:

This book is copyright protected. It is only for personal use. You cannot amend, distribute, sell, use, quote or paraphrase any part, or the content within this book, without the consent of the author or publisher.

Disclaimer Notice:

Please note the information contained within this document is for educational and entertainment purposes only. All effort has been executed to present accurate, up to date, reliable, complete information. No warranties of any kind are declared or implied. Readers acknowledge that the author is not engaged in the rendering of legal, financial, medical or professional advice. The content within this book has been derived from various sources. Please consult a licensed professional before attempting any techniques outlined in this book.
By reading this document, the reader agrees that under no circumstances is the author responsible for any losses, direct or indirect, that are incurred as a result of the use of the information contained within this document, including, but not limited to, errors, omissions, or inaccuracies.

Table of Content

Introduction 7

The Fundamentals of Whole Body Reset . 8

    The Middle Ages 8

    How Our Bodies and Nutritional Needs Change in Midlife and Beyond 9

    Dispeling Myths Surroundind Age, Nutrition, And Metabolism 12

    About Protein Timing 14

Breakfast and Smoothie Recipes 17

    Coconut Barley Porridge 17

    Veggie Quiche 17

    Toast Breakfast with Avocado 17

    Sesame Spelt Bread 17

    Overnight Chocolate-Blueberry Oatmeal ... 18

    Blueberry Cake 18

    Berry-Spinach Smoothies 18

    Mushroom-Bell Pepper Omelet 18

    Clam and Vegetable Chowder 19

    Awesome White Sandwich Bread 19

    Avocado Blueberry Smoothie 19

    Make-Ahead Smoothie 20

    Low-Carb Blueberry Smoothie 20

    Scrambled Tofu and Veggies 20

    Awesome Sweet Potato Salad 20

    Gingered Zucchini Bacon 21

    Avocado Tomato Pasta 21

    Carrot Cantaloupe Smoothie Bowl 21

    Blueberry Multigrain Pancakes 21

    Triple Berry Smoothie 22

    Bagels Made Healthy 22

    Simple Lime Watercress Salad 22

    Zucchini-Banana Bread Pancakes 22

    Apple Pumpkin Smoothie 23

    Orange-Carrot Smoothie 23

    Vegan Chocolate Smoothie 23

    Berry-Banana Smoothie with Almonds 23

    Almond Butter Chocolate Shake 24

    Banana-Peanut Butter 24

    Honey Green Tea Smoothie 24

    Protein Mango Smoothie 24

    Cauliflower-Melon Smoothies 24

    Savory Tomato-Bean Soup 25

    Banana Breakfast Shake 25

    Ulli's Granola 25

    Whey Berry Spinach Chia Smoothie 25

    Cantaloupe-Amaranth Smoothie 26

    Raisins-Plume Smoothie 26

    Apple-Banana Smoothie 26

    Avocado Spinach Smoothie 26

    Healthy Breakfast Sandwich 26

    Zucchini Bread 27

    Strawberry-Orange Smoothies 27

    Ginger-Pear Smoothie 27

    Mango And Cucumber Smoothie 27

    Cereal With Cranberry-Orange Twist 28

    Whole-Wheat Pretzels 28

    Nori Clove Smoothies 28

    Garbanzo Squash Smoothie 28

    Tamarind-Pear Smoothie 29

    Scrumptious Breakfast Salad 29

    Mediterranean Toast 29

    Green Protein Smoothie 29

    Almond Butter Cherry Smoothie 30

    Morning Smoothie 30

    Healthy Strawberry Smoothie 30

    Currant Elderberry Smoothie 30

    Matcha Smoothie 30

    Kale and Sweet Potato Hash 31

    Brazil Lettuce Smoothies 31

    Apple Pancakes 31

    Muesli Scones 31

    Strawberry-Kiwifruit Smoothies 32

Chewy Breakfast Cookies 32
Spinach-Grapefruit Smoothie 32
No-Cook Overnight Oats....................... 32

Vegan and Vegetarian Recipes..............33

Herbed Irish Stew 33
Brown Lentils..................................... 33
Awesome Mushroom Stroganoff 33
Basil-Spinach Lasagna 34
Chocolate Zucchini Brownies.................. 34
Vegan Jalapeno Poppers and Mushrooms .. 35
Mayo Mushroom Sandwich..................... 35
Vanilla Mug Brownie 36
Chocolate Mug Cake 36
Vegan Au Gratin Potatoes...................... 36
Baked Vegan Pancakes 37
Mayo Vegan Coleslaw 37
Lemony Vanilla Cake 37
Lemony Artichokes 38
Simple Carrots.................................... 38
Savory Almond Paste 38
Fried Jalapeno Cornbread 39
Blueberry Muffins 39
Orange Cake 39
Herbed Mushroom Stuffing 40
Gingerbread Cookies............................ 40
Vegan Cashew Macaroni and Cheese........ 41
Basil Oatmeal Patties 41

Salads and Sides Recipes......................42

Lemony Greek Salad............................ 42
Cucumber and Quinoa Tabbouleh 42
Mayo Pasta Salad................................ 42
Broccoli-Crab Salad with Rotini............... 43
Salmon-Shallot Pasta Salad 43
Lemony Almond-Arugula Salad................ 43
Tortellini and Veggies Salad 44
Lemony Shrimp Salad with Pasta Shell 44
Pomegranate Walnut Salad.................... 44

Sesame Tomato, Cucumber, and Quinoa Salad 45
Sesame Almonds, Strawberry, and Spinach Salad 45
Cauliflower & Eggs Salad....................... 45
Asparagus-Quinoa Salad 45
Avocado-Cobb Salad............................ 46
Basil Fiesta Salad................................ 46
Spinach Bean Soup 47
Vegetable-Barley Soup 47
Tomato Basil Soup 47
Turkey & Vegetable Barley Soup 47
Mint Almond-Quinoa Tabbouleh............... 48
Lemony Tuna Tomato Salad 48
Spinach Loaded Salad.......................... 48
Avocado Side Salad............................. 48
Grilled Asparagus-Spinach Salad 49
Beans and Corn Salad.......................... 49
Chicken and Greens Salads 49
Tasty Celery Root Salad 50
Dijon Red Leaf Salad 50
Kale, White Been & Tomato Sorghum Soup 50
Cauliflower Lunch Salad 51
Squid And Shrimp Salad 51
Curried Seven-Layer Salad 51
Beef Salad Topping 52
Rice and Peas Salad 52
Ranch-Barbecue Chicken Salad 52
Mayo Chicken Salad 53
Shrimp Salad with Cilantro Vinaigrette 53
Tabbouleh Salad 54
Avocado, Tomato, And Olives Salad 54
Radish And Olives Salad....................... 54
Marinated Carrot and Celery Salad 54
Tomato Green Bean Soup...................... 55
Potato-Fennel Soup 55
Spinach And Endives Salad................... 55
Radish and Tomato Salad...................... 55

Light Balsamic Salad............................ 56
Pesto Chicken & Cannellini Bean Soup...... 56
Vegetable Weight-Loss Soup.................... 56
Lemony Cucumber Salad........................ 57
Quinoa Cheese Salad 57
Curried Carrot & Apple Soup 57
Garden Vegetable Beef Soup.................... 58
Carrot Soup.. 58

Lunch Recipes 59

Sesame Flatbread Pizza........................... 59
Tuna Bites with Walnuts 59
Herbed Grain Burgers 59
Mushroom-Pepper Tacos 60
Marinated Portobello Burgers 60
Curried Eggplant with Quinoa.................. 60
Zoodles with Avocado Sauce 61
Crusted Salmon and Asparagus with Almonds 61
Stir-Fried Tofu and Green Beans............... 61
Southwest Tofu Scramble 62
Awesome Zucchini Hummus Wrap 62
Apple and Celery with Almonds 62
Spicy Shrimp Stir Fry.............................. 63
Superb Lemon Roasted Artichokes........... 63
Thai Seafood Soup 64
Shrimp and Zoodles................................ 64
Mushroom-Tomato Pasta 65
Peppered Kale 65
Chocolate Aquafaba Mousse.................... 65
Grilled Chicken Cobb Salad 66
Aromatic Salmon With Fennel Seeds 66
The OG Tuna Sandwich 66
Worcestershire Pork Chops 67
Greek Pork.. 67
Potato, Parsley, and Pumpkin Patties 67
Pork With Green Beans & Potatoes........... 67
Salmon And Beans Mix 68
Beef & Potatoes 68

Fried Rice with Veggies 68
Black-Eyed Peas And Greens Power Salad. 68
Rosemary Salmon 69
Black-Bean Soup.................................... 69
Simple Hummus 69
Pork And Chestnuts Mix 69
Spicy Ginger Seabass 70
Baked Potatoes And "BBQ" Lentils 70
Beef And Chili Mix 70
White Beans With Spinach And Pan-Roasted Tomatoes 70

Dinner Recipes 71

Spicy Chicken Nuggets............................ 71
Dijon Salmon 71
Enticing Grilled Tomatoes and Shrimp 71
Grilled Chicken Skewers......................... 72
Asian Chicken and Rice Dish 72
Shrimp-Stuffed Tomatoes with Spinach 72
Balsamic Chicken Breast 73
Slow Cooked Mediterranean Pork 73
Fried Mahi Mahi Bites............................. 73
Salmon With Salsa 74
Balsamic Grilled Basa 74
Italian Instant Pot Fish............................ 74
Balearic Beef Brisket Bowl 75
Especial Glazed Salmon 75
Healthy Vegetable Fried Rice 75
Chicken Meatloaf.................................... 76
Tahini Chicken Shawarma 76
Vegetarian Kebabs 76
Pork With Couscous............................... 77
Spanish Mussels 77
Cauliflower Mashed Potatoes................... 77
Avocado Tuna Cucumber Roll.................. 77
Balsamic Salmon Steaks 78
Broccoli With Garlic And Lemon............... 78
Salmon And Veggie Parcel 78
Garlic Shrimp Etouffee 79

Mahi Mahi Taco 79
Oregano Chicken Tacos Salad 80
Mackerel And Orange Medley 80
Mediterranean Lamb Chops 80
Lemongrass Shrimp/Chicken Soup 81
Brown Rice Pilaf 81
Lemony Shrimp with Cocktail Sauce 81

Snack and Appetizer Recipes 82

Garlic Salsa 82
Curried Almonds with Turmeric 82
Hoisin Button Mushrooms 82
Mexican Meat Dip 83
Veggie and Cheese Dip 83
Almond, Cranberry, and Coconut 83
Spicy Prairie Fire Dip 84
Awesome Seven-Layer Dip 84
Herbed Pizza Dip 84
Gingered Nuts Mix 85
Savory Balsamic Sausage Bites 85
Garlic Chicken Lettuce Wraps 85
Cornbread Pancakes 86
Creamy Seafood Dip 86
Garlic Flaxseed Crackers 86
Nuts And Seed Bowls 86
Mayo Deviled Eggs with Veggies 87
Protein Pancakes 87
Dijon Stuffed Eggs 87
Fantastic Chex Mix 88
Unique Apple Butter 88
Protein Bars 88
Enticing Turkey-Quinoa Meatballs 89
Almond 'You Must Be 89
Hummus With Ground Lamb 89
Zucchini Protein Pancakes 90
Stuffed Avocado 90

Salad On A Stick 90
Sesame Seed Balls 90
White Bean Dip 91
Lemony Artichokes 91
Eggplant Dip 91
Date Balls 91
Veggie Fritters 92
Protein-Rich Vegan Pancakes 92
Olive Tapenade With Anchovies 92
Smoked Salmon Crudités 93
Marinated Feta And Artichokes 93
Citrus-Marinated Olives 93
Boiled Unshelled Peanuts 93
Tuna Croquettes 94

Desserts 95

Chocolate Protein Muffins 95
Protein Pumpkin Muffins 95
Protein Bites 95
Protein Truffles 96
Banana Pie 96
"Chocolate" Pudding 96
Vegan Mango Ice Cream with Brazil Nuts .. 96
Strawberry-Applesauce Nice Cream 97
Almond Paleo Date Cookies 97
Blackberry Jam 97
Wrapped Plums 97
Homemade Whipped Cream 98
Chocolate Chip Oatmeal Protein Cookies ... 98
Mile-High Apple Pie 98

Conclusion 99

Appendix Measurement Conversion Chart
.... 100

Introduction

The Whole Body Reset is a science-based, tried-and-true program that targets weight gain and muscle loss associated with aging.

The Whole Body Reset: Your Weight-Loss Plan for a Flat Belly, Optimum Health & a Body You'll Love at Midlife and Beyond, is a weight-loss plan for a flat belly, optimum health, and a body you'll love at midlife and beyond.

Putting on weight as you get older isn't required. The Whole Body Reset explains why traditional diet and exercise advice stops working for us as we approach middle age—and shows how simple dietary changes can prevent and even heal age-related weight gain and muscle loss.

The Whole Body Reset presents groundbreaking new research on the benefits of "protein timing" for people in their forties and beyond, research that debunks current government guidelines, dispels the myth of slowing metabolisms and "inevitable" weight gain, and shifts how people in their forties and beyond should think about food.

The Whole Body Reset explains how our bodies change as we age and how eating to accommodate those changes can help us respond to exercise as if we were twenty to thirty years younger in simple, interesting language.

The Whole Body Reset, designed by AARP and reviewed by a panel of more than 100 AARP workers before being approved by an international board of doctors, nutritionists, and fitness experts, does not involve diet phases, eating windows, calorie restriction, or other trendy gimmicks.

Its six simple secrets and dozens of recipes are easy to follow and were developed with real people in mind. Even well-known eateries like McDonald's, Starbucks, and Olive Garden provide meal instructions that demonstrate how to follow this program. And, most importantly, it is effective!

About the Creator

As an author, editor, or publisher, Stephen Perrine has worked on more than two dozen New York Times bestsellers, including the Eat This, Not That! Series. He is in charge of health and wellness content for AARP the Magazine and the AARP Bulletin, which have a combined readership of over 38 million people.

He co-wrote Pretty Intense with Danica Patrick and co-created Better Man, a male-focused health and wellness TV show that is extensively syndicated. He has appeared on Dr. Oz, Today, Good Morning America, and the 700 Club as a nutrition expert. He was previously the editor-in-chief of Best Life and Men's Health's creative editorial director.

The Fundamentals of Whole Body Reset

The Middle Ages

The period between the ages of thirty-one and fifty is known as middle age. The beginning of this stage differs significantly from the finish. Many women, for example, experience pregnancy, childbirth, and nursing throughout their early middle years. Perimenopause, or the transition period leading up to menopause, or the end of menstruation, affects women in their later years of life. In the middle years of life, a number of physical changes occur, including the loss of bone mass in women due to low estrogen levels after menopause. Visual acuity drops in both men and women as they get older, and by the age of forty, they may be unable to see objects up close, a condition known as presbyopia. All of these things are symptoms of aging, as the human body changes in subtle and not-so-subtle ways. A middle-aged individual, on the other hand, can maintain vitality, health, and physical fitness by eating well and exercising regularly.

During this stage of the human life cycle, adults begin to encounter the first external signs of aging. Wrinkles begin to emerge, joints ache after a highly active day, and body fat increases. In the connective tissue, there is also a loss of muscle tone and flexibility. Many persons in their late thirties and forties experience a loss of endurance, the start of wear-and-tear injuries (such as osteoarthritis), and digestive system abnormalities. Wounds and other types of injuries take time to heal as well. Changes in body composition are caused by fat accumulation in the trunk. Maintaining health and wellness throughout your middle years and beyond requires:

- Maintaining a healthy body weight
- Eating nutrient-dense meals
- Drinking alcohol moderately or not at all
- Not smoking
- Engaging in moderate physical exercise for at least 150 minutes per week

Macronutrients and Energy

Women's energy requirements range from 1,800 to 2,200 calories while men's energy requirements range from 2,200 to 3,000 calories, depending on activity level. Women who are pregnant or breastfeeding are not included in these figures. To achieve these needs, middle-aged folks must rely on nutritious food sources. The typical eating habits in many places in North America do not correspond to the recommended guidelines. More than half of all vegetable consumption is made up of iceberg lettuce, frozen potatoes, fresh potatoes, potato chips, and canned tomatoes, for example. In the middle years of life, following dietary standards offers appropriate but not excessive energy, macronutrients, vitamins, and minerals.

From young adulthood until middle life, the AMDRs for carbs, protein, fat, fiber, and water stays constant. It's vital to avoid gaining weight and limiting SoFAAS intake to help prevent cardiovascular disease, diabetes, and other chronic illnesses.

Micronutrients

However, there are some distinctions in terms of micronutrients. Magnesium consumption for men should be increased to 420 milligrams per day, while magnesium intake for middle-aged women should be increased to 320 milligrams per day. Folate, vitamins B6 and B12, and other critical vitamins needed during middle age include folate and vitamins B6 and B12 to avoid an increase in homocysteine, a metabolic byproduct that can damage arterial walls and contribute to atherosclerosis, a cardiovascular disease. If you can't satisfy your nutrient needs through food, supplementation, such as a daily multivitamin, is recommended.

Nutrition that is both Preventative and Defensive

Preventive nutrition can improve wellbeing and assist organ systems functioning efficiently throughout aging in the middle years. Dietary practices aimed at minimizing disease and increasing health and well-being are referred to as preventive nutrition. Healthy dietary habits in general, such as choosing unrefined carbs over-processed carbohydrates and avoiding trans and saturated fats, contribute to overall wellness. There are, however, some things that people can do to address specific issues. Consuming antioxidant-rich foods, such as strawberries, blueberries, and other colored fruits and vegetables, can help to reduce cancer risk.

Phytochemicals are also excellent non-essential nutrients that may help to improve overall health. Carotenoids, which are found in carrots, cantaloupes, sweet potatoes, and butternut squash, for example, may protect against cardiovascular disease by preventing cholesterol oxidation in the arteries, though further research is needed.

Some studies suggest that lycopene, a phytochemical contained in watermelons and tomatoes, may protect against stomach, lung, and prostate cancer, according to the American Cancer Society, though further research is needed.

Omega-3 fatty acids have been demonstrated to help with coronary artery disease prevention. These vital nutrients are found in oily fish such as salmon, mackerel, tuna, herring, cod, and halibut. Monounsaturated fats, which can be found in plant oils, avocados, peanuts, and pecans, are also important for optimal functioning.

Menopause

Women go through a distinct transition in their middle years that has a significant impact on their health. They start going through menopause in their late forties or early fifties. The ovaries gradually stop producing estrogen and progesterone, resulting in the cessation of menstruation. Hot flashes, nocturnal sweats, and mood swings are some of the most common menopausal symptoms. Menopause can cause a variety of physiological changes, including changes in body composition, such as weight gain in the abdomen area, as a result of hormonal changes. Due to the lack of female reproductive hormones, bone loss is another prevalent side effect of menopause. Bone weakening raises the risk of fractures, limiting mobility and the capacity to do daily duties like cooking, bathing, and dressing.

How Our Bodies and Nutritional Needs Change in Midlife and Beyond

Healthy aging encompasses a variety of factors, including proper nutrition, regular exercise, and the prevention of mental decline. Some of these may be more straightforward than others. Nature has a say in all of them, no matter how skillfully we perform our part.

While the outward indicators of aging are usually obvious, the internal changes our bodies go through as we age – slower metabolism, decreased muscle mass, weakening organ tissue, and decreased bone density — are less visible. These changes, however, are very real. Thankfully, their negative effects on our overall health and well-being can be reduced by making proper dietary and lifestyle changes.

It's not always easy for elderly people to meet their changing health demands. For example, most seniors burn many fewer calories than they did in their middle years due to lower metabolic rates and inactive behavior. At the same time, the risk of malnutrition increases due to a decreased ability to absorb key nutrients, dehydration, loss of appetite, loss of taste, trouble swallowing, and other factors.

Every decade reduces energy requirements, but the issue is to eat more nutrient-dense meals while eating less overall.

The truth is that as we age, our bodies require the same amount of protein, vitamins, and minerals as they did when we were younger, if not more. For example, around the age of 50, the ability to absorb critical nutrients such as vitamins B12 or D gradually deteriorates due to decreased stomach acidity, which aids in the breakdown of these vitamins. The remedy is to consume foods that are high in these nutrients.

It isn't just the digestive system that deteriorates. The ability of aging skin to convert vitamin D from sunshine decreases, which reduces calcium absorption, an essential nutrient to prevent bone loss. Older persons should take daily multivitamin and mineral supplements for these and other reasons.

Another issue that worsens with age is the risk of dehydration. Because regulatory processes aren't as keen as they were in the early years, an older person may not feel thirsty even if he or she is dehydrated to the point of dehydration. The remedy is to make it a habit to drink six 8-ounce glasses of water every day, regardless of thirst.

Lack of access to healthy food is one of the leading causes of malnutrition among the elderly. Getting to a grocery shop may be too difficult, especially if driving is no longer an option. It's possible that cooking facilities are unavailable or too difficult to use. It could be a lack of appetite, forgetfulness, or motivation as a result of loneliness or depression. However, missing meals for any reason has severe health consequences and can result in major nutritional harm.

The ideal option would be to spend time making and eating meals with family and friends. This allows family members to keep a watch on an elderly person's eating habits. Meals on Wheels, for example, can help fill in some of the gaps. Unfortunately, aging is connected with increased social isolation and isolation for far too many people, which can have far-reaching negative consequences on multiple levels. This does not need to be the case.

What Effects Does Aging Have on Your Nutritional Needs?

A multitude of changes in the body is associated with aging, including muscle loss, thinner skin, and lower stomach acid.

Some of these changes may put you at risk for vitamin deficiencies, while others may have an impact on your senses and overall quality of life. According to studies, 20% of senior persons suffer from atrophic gastritis, a disorder in which persistent inflammation damages the cells that create stomach acid.

Low stomach acid can prevent nutrients including vitamin B12, calcium, iron, and magnesium from being absorbed.

Another problem that people face as they get older is a reduction in their calorie requirements. Unfortunately, this results in a nutritional conundrum. While eating fewer calories, older folks require just as much, if not more, of some nutrients. Fortunately, you may meet your nutrient needs by eating a range of healthy foods and taking a supplement.

Another concern that people may face as they become older is a decrease in their body's ability to perceive key feelings such as hunger and thirst. Dehydration and unintended weight loss may result as a result of this. And as you become older, these impacts may become more severe.

Aging is associated with muscle loss, thinner skin, and reduced stomach acid. As you get older, your capacity to distinguish hunger and thirst may deteriorate.

Fewer Calories Are Required, but More Nutrients

The daily calorie requirements of an individual are determined by their height, weight, muscle mass, activity level, and a variety of other factors.

Because they move and exercise less and carry less muscle, older folks may require fewer calories to maintain their weight.

You will acquire weight if you continue to consume the same number of calories per day as you did when you were younger, especially around your midsection.

This is especially true in postmenopausal women, as the drop in estrogen levels that occurs during this time may encourage the storage of belly fat.

Even though older folks require fewer calories, they require the same or even higher levels of some nutrients than younger ones.

For older people, this emphasizes the need of eating a variety of whole meals such fruits, vegetables, fish, and lean meats. These nutrient-dense staples can help you combat nutrient deficiency without adding inches to your waistline.

Protein, vitamin D, calcium, and vitamin B12 are all nutrients that become increasingly vital as you get older.

In general, older folks require fewer calories. Their dietary needs, on the other hand, are the same as or greater than when they were younger. As a result, eating nutrient-dense, whole meals becomes critical.

You Can Benefit from Increasing Your Protein Intake

As you become older, you're likely to lose muscle and strength.

In reality, beyond the age of 30, the average adult loses 3–8% of their muscle mass per decade.

Sarcopenia is the term for a decrease in muscle mass and strength.

It's a leading cause of senior frailty, fractures, and poor health.

More protein in your diet may assist your body to maintain muscle mass and combat sarcopenia.

Over the course of three years, a study tracked 2,066 elderly persons. It was shown that persons who ate the most protein per day lost 40% less muscle mass than those who ate the least.

In addition, a review of 20 recent research in senior persons indicated that increasing protein intake or using protein supplements can help halt muscle loss, enhance muscle mass, and aid in muscle growth.

Furthermore, the most effective strategy to combat sarcopenia appears to be combining a protein-rich diet with resistance training.

Sarcopenia, or the age-related loss of muscle and strength, maybe aided by a high-protein diet. According to research, combining a protein-rich diet with resistance exercise may provide the best results.

You May Benefit from More Fiber

Constipation is a prevalent health issue among senior citizens.

It's more common in persons over 65, and women are two to three times more likely than men.

This is due to the fact that persons in their forties and fifties tend to walk less and are more prone to take drugs with constipation as a side effect.

Constipation can be relieved by eating fiber. It passes through the intestines undigested, assisting in the formation of stool and the maintenance of regular bowel movements.

Dietary fiber helped increase bowel movements in persons with constipation, according to a review of five research.

Diverticular disease is a disorder in which tiny pouches grow along the colon wall and become infected or inflamed. A high-fiber diet may help prevent this. This is a very common ailment among the elderly.

Diverticular illness is sometimes misunderstood as a condition caused by a Western diet. It's extremely common, with up to 50% of persons over the age of 50 in Western countries suffering from it.

Diverticular illness, on the other hand, is nearly non-existent in people who consume more fiber. Diverticular illness, for example, affects less than 0.2 percent of persons in Japan and Africa.

As you get older, you may experience bowel problems such as constipation and diverticular disease. Increasing your fiber intake can help you protect yourself.

More Calcium and Vitamin D Are Required

Two of the most critical minerals for bone health are calcium and vitamin D.

Calcium aids in the formation and maintenance of healthy bones, whereas vitamin D aids in calcium absorption.

Unfortunately, elderly persons have a lower ability to absorb calcium from their food.

According to human and animal studies, the intestine absorbs less calcium as we become older. However, because aging might make the body less efficient at making vitamin D, the decline in calcium absorption is most likely due to a vitamin D deficit.

When your skin is exposed to sunshine, your body can produce vitamin D from the cholesterol in your skin. However, as people age, their skin becomes thinner, reducing their ability to produce vitamin D.

These changes may prevent you from getting enough calcium and vitamin D, leading to bone loss and an increased risk of fracture.

It's vital to take more calcium and vitamin D through foods and supplements to counteract the effects of aging on your vitamin D and calcium levels.

Calcium is found in a range of foods, including dairy products and dark green, leafy vegetables. Vitamin D, on the other hand, can be found in a variety of seafood, including salmon and herring. Vitamin D supplementation, such as cod liver oil, may also be beneficial to the elderly.

Calcium and vitamin D are essential elements for healthy bone health. As you get older, your body will benefit from additional calcium and vitamin D.

You Might Require More Vitamin B12 (Cobalamin)

Cobalamin, often known as vitamin B12, is a water-soluble vitamin.

It's required for the production of red blood cells and the maintenance of normal brain function.

Unfortunately, research shows that 10–30% of persons over the age of 50 have a reduced ability to absorb vitamin B12 from food.

This could lead to a vitamin B12 deficit over time. Vitamin B12 is attached to proteins in the foods you eat in your diet. Stomach acid must aid it separate from these dietary proteins before it can be used by your body.

In older persons, diseases that limit stomach acid production are more common, resulting in lower vitamin B12 absorption from meals. One disorder that can cause this is atrophic gastritis.

Furthermore, because vitamin B12 is more prevalent in animal foods like eggs, fish, meat, and dairy, elderly individuals who adopt a vegan or vegetarian diet are less likely to consume high-quality supplies of the vitamin.

As a result, elderly persons may benefit from taking a vitamin B12 supplement or eating vitamin B12-fortified foods.

The crystalline vitamin B12 in these fortified foods is not linked to dietary proteins. As a result, persons who produce less stomach acid than normal can nevertheless absorb it.

As people get older, vitamin B12 insufficiency becomes more common. Taking a vitamin B12 supplement or eating foods fortified with vitamin B12 can be especially beneficial to older persons.

Other Nutrients to Consider as You Grow Older

Other nutrients that may be beneficial as you get older include:

- **Potassium:** A higher potassium consumption is linked to a reduced risk of high blood pressure, kidney stones, osteoporosis, and heart disease, all of which are more prevalent in the elderly.
- **Omega-3 fatty acids:** The major cause of death among the elderly is heart disease. Omega-3 fatty acids have been demonstrated in studies to reduce heart disease risk factors such as high blood pressure and triglycerides.
- **Magnesium:** Magnesium is a crucial nutrient for the human body. Unfortunately, due to low intake, medication use, and age-related changes in gastrointestinal function, elderly adults are at risk of deficiency.
- **Iron:** Deficiency is widespread among the elderly. Anemia, a disorder in which the blood does not give enough oxygen to the body, may result as a result of this.

A diet rich in fruits, vegetables, seafood, and lean meats can provide the majority of these nutrients. People who eat a vegetarian or vegan diet, on the other hand, may benefit from taking an iron or omega-3 supplement.

Although iron can be found in a number of vegetables, plant-based iron is not as readily absorbed as meat-based iron. Fish is the main source of omega-3 fats.

Other nutrients that can help you age gracefully include potassium, magnesium, omega-3 fatty acids, and iron.

You Have a Higher Risk of Dehydration

Water makes up roughly 60% of your body weight.

It's critical to stay hydrated at any age since your body loses water on a regular basis, primarily through sweat and urine.

Additionally, as you become older, you may become more prone to dehydration.

Thirst is detected by receptors located in the brain and throughout the body.

These receptors may become less sensitive to water changes as you get older, making it more difficult for them to detect thirst.

Your kidneys also help your body save water, although they lose function as you get older.

Dehydration, however, has major consequences for the elderly.

Long-term dehydration reduces the fluid in your cells, making it harder to take drugs, exacerbating medical disorders, and increasing weariness.

As a result, it's critical to make a conscious effort to drink adequate water on a daily basis.

If you have trouble drinking water, try consuming one to two glasses with each meal. Otherwise, carry a water bottle with you throughout the day.

Drinking plenty of water becomes more important as you become older, because your body may lose its ability to detect dehydration.

You May Struggle to Consume Enough Food

Another source of concern for the elderly is a loss of appetite.

If this problem isn't fixed, it can result in unexpected weight loss and nutritional deficits. Appetite loss has also been related to ill health and a higher chance of mortality.

Changes in hormones, taste, and smell, as well as changes in life circumstances, can all contribute to a loss of appetite in older persons.

According to studies, older adults have lower amounts of hunger hormones and higher levels of fullness hormones, which implies they may eat less frequently and feel filled faster.

Researchers discovered that elderly people had much lower levels of the hunger hormone ghrelin before a meal in a short trial involving 11 elderly people and 11 young adults.

Furthermore, multiple investigations have discovered that the fullness hormones cholecystokinin and leptin are increased in aged adults.

Aging can impair your sense of smell and taste, making foods less appetizing.

Tooth loss, loneliness, underlying sickness, and appetite-suppressing drugs are all possible causes of decreased appetite.

If eating large meals is difficult for you, try breaking your meals into smaller amounts and eating them every few hours.

Otherwise, try to make a practice of snacking on nutritious foods like almonds, yogurt, and boiled eggs, which are high in minerals and calories.

It's not uncommon for elderly folks to have a loss of appetite. If not addressed, this problem can result in weight loss, nutritional deficits, and bad health.

Deficits in calcium, vitamin D, vitamin B12, iron, magnesium, and other critical minerals can occur as a result of aging.

It may also impair your capacity to notice basic bodily sensations such as hunger and thirst.

You can, however, take precautions to avoid these errors.

Make an effort to keep track of your water and food intake, consume a range of nutrient-dense foods, and think about taking a supplement.

All of these acts can assist you in overcoming inadequacies and maintaining your health as you age.

Dispeling Myths Surroundind Age, Nutrition, And Metabolism

Myths About Nutrition and Aging Debunked
Although people are living longer, their quality of life is deteriorating. After the age of 65, the disease load increases significantly. As a result, older persons are more likely to take many drugs, increasing their risk of frailty and death.

This, however, does not have to be the case. Chronic diseases have strong roots in lifestyle choices, such as food. It's possible to shed some light on healthy aging by dispelling some popular beliefs about diet and nutrition among older persons.

Myth #1: You Only Need a Smaller Amount of Food
As people age, their muscular mass declines, resulting in fewer energy demands. However, staying active and maintaining strong muscles are vital for maintaining good bone density. Even if a slowed metabolism lowers calorie requirements, older folks require more nutrients and fiber from a variety of whole meals than ever before to stay healthy.

Myth #2: Skipping Meals Is Okay
Taste and smell can deteriorate with age, affecting appetite. However, missing meals might send you into a downward spiral. It has the potential to reduce blood sugar levels and raise the risk of malnutrition. If you're hungry, consume sweet fruit, season meals with salt and herbs, and eat small portions and frequent snacks with high nutrition density to ensure your protein demands are satisfied.

Myth #3: Nutritional Supplements Will Fix Things
Supplements will never be able to replace the whole range of vitamins, minerals, protein, healthy fats, polyphenols, and fiber that a whole food diet provides. However, they are sometimes required to supplement a healthy diet. B12 and Vitamin D are the vitamins that are most vulnerable to aging. If your hunger is poor, protein smoothies can give a concentrated source of protein.

Myth #4: Being Overweight is Fine
Obesity and overweight raise the risk of chronic disease at any age, even if a little extra padding is acceptable in later years. For better health, older persons who are overweight should lose 5-10 percent of their body weight over 6 months. Eating natural meals and avoiding overly processed foods with refined carbohydrates and harmful fats is the best way.

Myth #5: If Your Weight is Okay, You Can Eat Everything You Want
While being overweight or underweight can cause a slew of health issues, those who are in the average weight range can also suffer from bad health. Chronic inflammation, which is linked to a variety of physical and mental health issues, can be caused by an improper diet. At any age or weight, a whole food, low-processed-food diet is essential.

Myth #6: Let Thirst Guide Your Fluid Intake
Thirst is not always a good indicator of fluid demands, especially as people age and their thirst sense fade. Dehydration is an often-overlooked condition among older persons for this and other reasons. It can result in ill health, hospitalization, or even death. Dehydration, even slight dehydration, can result in weakness, dizziness, low blood pressure, and an increased risk of falling. Make sure you have plenty of fluids on hand, especially water and herbal tea.

Myth #7: It's Normal to Get Sick as You Get Older
Being unwell is not normal, despite the fact that bodily parts wear out over time. Excellent nutrition, regular hydration, a healthy weight, physical activity, mental stimulation, social interaction, and careful management of any needless medications can all contribute to good health.

Myth #8: Senility is Unavoidable
Dementia risk is linked to a number of lifestyle variables, including inactivity and a poor diet. A Mediterranean-style diet, which is high in plant foods and healthy fats, with moderate amounts of fish and dairy and low intakes of red meat and processed foods, has been shown to be beneficial in studies. B vitamins, antioxidants (found in plant-based diets), and omega-3 fatty acids may all aid to reduce dementia risk.

Metabolism and Age: Researchers Debunk Myths about Calorie Burning in Late Adulthood
Although it is widely assumed that a person's calorie-burning potential peaks during adolescence, a new study suggests that the body's metabolism process begins to deteriorate later in life.

After analyzing the average number of calories burned by more than 6,600 people from 29 different nations as they went about their daily lives, an international team of experts came to that conclusion. The findings of the research were published in the journal Science, with individuals ranging in age from one week to 95 years old.

Jennifer Rood, the study's co-author, said in a statement that "as we age, there are a number of physiological changes that occur in the phases of our lives such as during puberty and menopause."

Rood expressed her surprise that the timing of our metabolism "doesn't appear to fit the markers we connect with growing up and getting older" while presenting the study.

Metabolism is a physiological process in which the body transforms food into energy. Previous studies have estimated how much energy the body expends on basic tasks like breathing and pumping blood, but scientists estimate that only 50 to 70% of the calories we burn each day are spent on these activities.

Researchers employed a urine test known as the "doubly labeled water" method to determine how much energy a person requires during the day. The test asks a person to consume a glass of water with "naturally occurring heavy forms" in place of hydrogen and oxygen molecules. By observing how rapidly the forms are flushed out, researchers can calculate a person's energy expenditure.

Since the 1980s, the doubly labeled water method has been regarded as the gold standard for quantifying daily energy expenditure, but the test's expensive cost has limited the scale and scope of prior investigations. Multiple labs shared their data to see if they might expand on their study to avoid this problem.

According to the research, kids have an initial burst of calorie-burning and energy needs during infancy that lowers by roughly 3% each year until they reach their 20s when it begins to level off. By their first birthdays, newborns are burning 50 percent more calories than adults for their body size.

In a statement, Peter Katzmarzyk of the Pennington Biomedical Research Center (PBRC) in Baton Rouge, La. said, "Some people think of their teens and 20s as the age when their calorie-burning potential reaches its zenith." "However, the study found that babies had the highest metabolic rates of all."

Children that are malnourished throughout this developmental stage are less likely to survive and grow up to be healthy adults, which could be explained by their high metabolism.

"To have a greater understanding of a baby's metabolism, more research is required. We need to figure out what is causing increased energy costs "According to the PBRC's Corby Martin.

People's metabolism levels after puberty were mostly steady from their 20s to their 50s, according to scientists, and calorie needs climbed no more than expected throughout pregnancy.

According to the research, our metabolism does not begin to fall again until we reach the age of 60, and even then, the decline is moderate, at 0.7 percent every year.

Meanwhile, experts claim that people in their 90s require 26% fewer calories per day than typical older people. This could be linked to aging-related muscle loss, but scientists say there's more to look into.

Adult Metabolism is Steady until the Age of 60, According to a New Study

The concept that metabolism slows as people become older has been debunked by a big study that evaluated the overall amount of energy expended by people as they go about their daily lives.

According to the study, total energy expenditure reduces constantly from a high in childhood until around the age of 20, then stabilizes until around the age of 60. Only then does energy consumption begin to decrease.

The researchers were startled to see that, despite their small size, 1-year-olds burn 50 percent more calories than adults.

Dr. Herman Pontzer, associate professor of evolutionary anthropology and global health at Duke University in Durham, NC, says, "Of course, they're growing, but even if you compensate for that, their energy expenditures are rocketing up higher than you'd expect for their body size and composition."

According to Dr. Pontzer, puberty and menopause are two physiological turning points that come with getting older.

"What's strange is that our metabolic life phases' don't seem to correspond to those usual milestones," he explains.

Another surprise was the lack of variation in energy expenditure from early adulthood to middle life.

"Perhaps the most surprising characteristic was the consistency of metabolic rate in both boys and females between the ages of 20 and 60," co-author Dr. John Speakman of the University of Aberdeen in the United Kingdom, tweeted.

"This shows that if you're having middle-age spread, it's more probable because you're consuming more than you're expending," he continued.

Doubly Labeled Water

The data was analyzed by an international team of academics who looked at the total energy expenditure of 6,421 people aged from 8 days to 95 years old who lived in 29 different countries.

In the past, most energy expenditure research has concentrated on resting or basal metabolism, or the number of calories burned simply to keep the body running.

The energy that the body spends on vital tasks like breathing, digesting food, and pumping blood around the body is referred to as basal metabolism.

However, this only accounts for 50–70% of all calories consumed by humans. It excludes, for example, common but energetic activities such as walking, climbing stairs, jogging, or grocery shopping.

The new study's authors chose a different strategy, employing "doubly labeled water," the gold standard scientific technique for determining total energy expenditure.

This method necessitates the consumption of water containing uncommon isotopes (heavier versions) of hydrogen and oxygen atoms by study participants.

Researchers next examine daily urine samples from each participant to determine the rate at which each isotope is excreted.

The difference between the two elimination rates indicates how much carbon dioxide the person produces, which in turn indicates how quickly they burn calories.

Researchers have been using doubly tagged water to track how many calories people burn as they go about their regular activities since the 1980s. The exorbitant cost of the oxygen isotope, however, has limited the scope of such research. The current study circumvented this constraint by compiling data from a variety of studies from around the world into a single database.

Waxing and Waning Metabolism

The very high metabolic rate seen in the tissues of neonates, according to scientists, may be related to their rapid growth and development.

Reduced energy expenditure in elderly people, on the other hand, might be a sign of a slowing of organ metabolism.

The researchers anticipate that the metabolic changes they discovered will lead to more research into illness development, drug activity, and healing, all of which are closely linked to metabolic rate.

Furthermore, even after accounting for body composition, sex, and age, they found significant disparities in energy consumption among participants in their study.

One of the study's flaws was that it didn't include any information regarding possible relevant factors like food and physical activity.

The researchers come to the following conclusion: "Understanding the processes behind metabolic changes throughout time and individual variation might help elucidate the significance of metabolic variation in health and illness."

Studies in animals reveal that metabolic alterations are fundamental to the aging process, according to Timothy Rhoads and Rozalyn Anderson of the University of Wisconsin-School Madison's of Medicine and Public Health.

They express themselves as follows:

"A change in tissue-specific metabolism, or the energy expended on maintenance, is assumed to be the cause of the drop beyond 60." It can't be a coincidence that the rise in non-communicable disease and disorder incidence started around the same period."

"Cellular activity appears to be dropping beyond [60 years of age], but pinpointing which processes are changing is difficult," Dr. Pontzer told Medical News Today.

"I agree that maintenance and repair are declining, contributing to aging processes," he said, adding that "additional study is needed to pin that down."

About Protein Timing

Is Protein Timing Important for Muscle Growth?

Protein: What Is It and Why Is It Important?

A protein is a substance that the body uses to make tissues, hormones, enzymes, and other life-sustaining chemicals.

It's made up of amino acids, which are the body's basic building blocks, which are chains of smaller molecules.

Protein is made up of 21 amino acids, of which your body can manufacture 12 but must obtain the remaining 9 from the diet.

These nine amino acids are regarded as essential amino acids and include:

- Phenylalanine
- Valine
- Threonine
- Tryptophan
- Methionine
- Leucine
- Isoleucine
- Lysine
- Histidine

Many plant and animal tissues are high in protein and can be used as a dietary source for the amino acids we require.

This is why you must consume protein: to ensure that your body receives enough vital amino acids. Your body requires more or less protein depending on a number of factors, including your age and degree of activity.

Because it damages tissues that must be regenerated, regular exercise, particularly weightlifting, raises the body's requirement for protein.

Although sedentary persons may not require as much protein as weightlifters, they do require more than the majority of people consume, and protein intake is more significant than most people realize.

The reason for this is that not getting enough protein promotes muscle loss as you age, and the less lean mass you have in your later years, the more likely you are to die from any cause.

The basic message is that you must retain your muscle mass as you age in order to keep your health.

A high-protein diet (together with resistance training) is essential for this.

Acids and enzymes in your stomach break down protein into amino acids when you eat it.

Some proteins, such as whey, break down fast, while others, such as eggs, take a long time.

The amino acids travel to the small intestine, where they are transported into the bloodstream by specific cells. They're then shuttled into cells all around your body to be used.

Now, because when you eat protein, many different processes happen in your body, let's reword the question to match the context of this discussion:
What effect does protein have on your muscles?
To grasp this, we must focus on leucine, one of the key amino acids in protein.
Because it directly increases protein synthesis, which is the process by which amino acids are ordered into proteins that can eventually be utilized for muscular building, leucine has a particular place in bodybuilders' hearts.
So...
1. You consume a food that contains protein, which is made up of linked amino acids.
2. Your body breaks those links in order to get the free amino acids it needs to make its own proteins.
3. The presence of leucine alerts the body that amino acids are accessible for usage and that protein synthesis can begin.
4. Your body responds by producing a pool of freshly formed proteins that it can employ to construct and repair tissues, including muscle tissue.
As you might expect, the amount of amino acids provided by a meal has an impact on the amount of muscle growth that can occur.
This is why studies have found that the amount of leucine in a meal has a direct impact on the amount of protein synthesis that happens as a result. In other words, meals high in leucine have a stronger muscle-building potential than meals low in leucine.
This is why it's critical to think about the quality of the protein you're consuming.
You want a protein that is easily absorbed by the body and is high in critical amino acids, particularly leucine.
Animal proteins, such as meat, eggs, and dairy, are extremely popular among bodybuilders since they meet all of these characteristics.
(This isn't to argue that a vegan can't gain muscle effectively.) If you know what you're doing, you can.)
So, now that we've covered the fundamentals of protein metabolism, we can go on to the topic at hand...

A Basic Science of Protein and Muscle Growth
Proteins are continually broken down and regenerated in all of your body's cells.
Of course, this applies to muscular tissue, and these breakdown and synthesis processes are functioning at all times, albeit to variable degrees.
When you're starved, for example, protein breakdown rates increase, and if they surpass synthesis rates, muscle loss occurs. A state of negative protein balance is referred to as this.
Protein synthesis increases when you eat protein, and when it exceeds breakdown rates, muscle gain occurs. This is referred to as a positive protein balance situation.

Every day, your body alternates between anabolic and catabolic stages in this manner.
Muscle tissue is relatively stable under typical health and dietary conditions, and the cellular regeneration cycle is balanced.
This is why the average individual does not gain or lose muscle mass quickly. There are no apparent variations in total lean mass on a daily basis. (That said, if we don't take steps to prevent it, we will lose lean mass as we age, but you get the idea.)
When we train our muscles, the cells in our muscle fibers are injured, causing the body to raise protein synthesis rates to repair the damage.
Our bodies are also intelligent, and they strive to adapt in order to cope better with the activities that produced the muscle damage. They do this by implanting cells into the muscle fibers.
This is how muscles develop their size and strength.
As a result, what we call "muscle growth" is actually the result of protein synthesis rates outpacing protein breakdown rates over time.
In other words, you build muscle when your body synthesizes (creates) more muscle proteins than it loses.
When it generates fewer than it loses, you've lost muscle.
And you haven't developed or lost muscle if it creates roughly the same number as it lost.
This is why bodybuilders go to great lengths to increase protein synthesis and decrease protein breakdown, using

- Eating a high-protein, high-carbohydrate diet
- In the gym, gradually overloading their muscles
- Checking to see if they're in a calorie deficit
- Nutrition before and after a workout
- Eating a protein-rich meal before going to bed
- Cutting back on cardio
- Supplementation
- Steroids and other medications (in many circumstances)

The goal is to keep protein synthesis rates as high as feasible above protein breakdown rates for as many hours as possible during the day.
As you can see, there are a lot of variables at play when it comes to determining whether you're adding or losing muscle.
Some are also more significant than others.
For example, eating protein before bed isn't nearly as crucial as getting enough protein throughout the day.
And this takes us to the article's fundamental question:
When it comes to protein timing, how essential is it? Does the frequency with which you consume protein have a significant impact on the balance between protein synthesis and breakdown (protein turnover)?

Does Proteins Timing Really Matter?
As I already stated, I used to be convinced that it did.

I was convinced that eating protein four to six times a day was essential for muscle building.

It's not critical, to be sure.

We can find solid proof of this in a research on the intermittent fasting strategy to dieting.

It's generally established that intermittent fasting (IF) does not result in muscle loss because it entails fasting (no food) for extended periods of time followed by anywhere from 2 to 8-hour "feeding windows."

One study indicated that ingesting the equivalent of a full day's worth of protein in a 4-hour window (followed by a 20-hour fast) did not result in muscle loss. Several additional investigations have come up with similar results.

The important line is that if you skip a meal or fail to give a steady supply of vital amino acids, your muscle will not wither.

You won't lose muscle if you eat adequate protein every day.

However, there is evidence that eating protein only 1 to 3 times per day is insufficient for muscle growth.

Let's start with a study conducted by RMIT University academics. It featured 24 fit young men who exercised and then consumed protein in one of three ways:

1. 4 servings of 20 grams of protein, separated by 3 hours.
2. 2 servings of 40 grams of protein, separated by 6 hours.
3. 8 servings of 10 grams of protein, separated by 1.5 hours.

And what was the end result?

Group 1 produced much more muscle protein than groups 2 and 3.

It's also worth highlighting a study undertaken by scientists at the University of Texas.

Protein synthesis was shown to be around 23% higher in those who ate three large meals containing 23 grams of protein with three smaller meals containing 15 grams of necessary amino acids than in people who ate only three large meals.

Athletes in a calorie deficit have experienced similar results.

When you consider what we know about how protein absorption influences protein metabolism, these findings aren't surprising.

Your body's ability to digest, process, and utilize protein for protein production is restricted.

According to research, the average person expends roughly 6 to 7 grams every hour (and it's likely significantly higher in people with above-average muscularity).

The amount of protein synthesis that can be induced by a single intake of protein has a limit.

This ceiling is known as the "muscle full effect," because once achieved, amino acids are no longer employed for muscle development and are instead targeted for removal (oxidation).

Researchers had young men ingest varied amounts of egg protein after an exercise in one trial and then assessed protein synthesis rates.

They came to the conclusion that 20 grams of protein was the top limit since it delivered 89% of the protein synthesis response that 40 grams did.

A comparable study utilizing whey protein revealed the same thing–20 grams was nearly as efficient as 40 grams at increasing protein synthesis rates.

A study that demonstrated no statistically significant difference in protein synthesis rates after 30 and 90 grams of ground beef intake reported similar results.

When you ingest protein, your protein synthesis rates can only stay elevated for a certain amount of time.

Regardless of how long amino acids remain in your bloodstream, muscle protein synthesis rates remain increased for no more than 3 hours, according to research.

To put it another way, a high amount of protein may take 6 to 7 hours to digest and process completely, yet protein synthesis rates will remain increased for only 3 of those hours.

So, if the body can only process about 7 grams of protein per hour for muscle protein synthesis......and if muscle protein synthesis lasts no longer than 3 hours......we can see why eating 30 grams of protein every 3 to 4 hours results in more muscle protein accumulation over time than eating fewer, larger servings separated by longer periods.

Increasing the frequency with which you consume protein...

- **You should try to keep protein synthesis rates above baseline for as many hours as feasible during the day.**

You allow the amino acids to be used predominantly for protein synthesis, with only a little portion set aside for oxidation.

To put it another way, you want to get the most muscle growth out of each meal and your diet as a whole.

The evidence is clear: the order in which proteins are consumed is crucial.

If you eat 4 to 6 servings of protein each day, you'll probably grow muscle faster than if you eat fewer.

However, unlike total protein consumption and progressive overload, it isn't a deal-breaker.

You can still gain muscle if you prefer to consume fewer, larger meals (as in intermittent fasting).

It's simply not the best approach to go about it.

Breakfast and Smoothie Recipes

Coconut Barley Porridge

Preparation time: 8 minutes
Cooking time: 5 minutes
Serves: 2

Ingredients
- 1 cup unsweetened coconut milk, divided
- 1 small banana, peeled and sliced
- ½ cup barley
- 3 drops liquid stevia
- ¼ cup coconuts, chopped

Instructions:
1. In a bowl, thoroughly combine the barley, stevia, and half the coconut milk. Cover and chill for around 6 hours.
2. In a saucepan, combine the barley mixture with the coconut milk. 5 minutes of cooking at medium heat.
3. Add banana slices and coconut shavings on top. Serve

Nutritional Info: Calories 336; Fat 8g; Sodium 68mg; Carbs 59g; Fiber 10g; Sugar 13.4g; Protein 9.7g

Veggie Quiche

Preparation time: 14 minutes
Cooking time: 4 hours
Serves: 4

Ingredients
- 1 cup garbanzos bean flour
- ¾ cup fresh coconut milk
- 1 tbsp sea salt
- 1 tbsp oregano
- ¼ teaspoon cayenne pepper
- 2 cups mushrooms, sliced
- 1 cup kale, chopped
- ½ cup white onions, chopped
- ½ cup yellow peppers, seeded and chopped

Instructions:
1. Combine the coconut milk, salt, oregano, and cayenne pepper with the garbanzo bean flour.
2. Make a smooth dough by mixing.
2. Mix together the remaining ingredients. Pour the ingredients into the Instant Pot's bottom-mounted parchment paper pan. Although the vent should not be in the sealing position, close the lid.
3. Choose Slow Cook and set the timer for 4 hours.

Nutritional Info: Calories 233; Fat 4.7g; Sodium 519mg; Carbs 37g; Fiber 7g; Sugar 8g; Protein 12g

Toast Breakfast with Avocado

Preparation time: 10 minutes
Cooking time: 15 minutes
Serves: 3

Ingredients
- 2 small sized sprouted bread
- 1 cup finely cut tomatoes
- 2 moderate avocados
- 1 small cup alfalfa
- Pure sea salt and bell pepper

Instructions:
1. Combine the bread with the avocado, alfalfa, and tomatoes.
2. Add pure sea salt and freshly ground pepper to taste. Eat a lavish breakfast and pair it with your favorite freshly squeezed juice.

Nutritional Info: Calories 261; Fat 20g; Sodium 52mg; Carbs 20g; Fiber 10g; Sugar 2.8g; Protein 4.6g

Sesame Spelt Bread

Preparation time: 8 minutes
Cooking time: 6 hours
Serves: 8

Ingredients
- 4-½ cups spelt flour
- 2 tsp sea salt
- 2 cups spring water
- ¼ cup agave
- Grapeseed oil for brushing the bread
- A dash of sesame seeds

Instructions:
1. To combine the ingredients, use the mixer's hook attachment. Combine the salt and spelt flour in a bowl. 10 seconds of mixing should be done in a mixer. Add the water and agave next. To create a dough, mix for ten minutes or longer.
2. Place the dough in a clean bowl after coating it with grapeseed oil. Give yourself at least an hour to rest. After that, line the Instant Pot's base with parchment paper.
3. Before placing the dough inside the Instant Pot, sprinkle it with sesame seeds. Although the vent should not be in the sealing position, close the lid.
4. Select "Slow Cook" and set the cooking period to six hours.

Nutritional Info: Calories 150; Fat 0.9g; Sodium 584mg; Carbs 30.5g; Fiber 1.3g; Sugar 0.2g; Protein 4.2g

Overnight Chocolate-Blueberry Oatmeal

Preparation time: 10 minutes
Cooking time: None
Serves: 2

Ingredients
- 1 cup unsweetened almond milk
- 1 cup rolled oats
- 1 tbsp cacao powder
- 8-10 drops liquid stevia
- ¼ cup fresh blueberries
- 1 tbsp unsweetened dark mini chocolate chips

Instructions:
1. In a large mixing bowl, combine all of the ingredients (except the blueberries and chocolate chips) and thoroughly combine. Overnight in the refrigerator, cover the bowl. Serve the dish with blueberries and chocolate chips on top.

Nutritional Info: Calories 233; Fat 6.4g; Sodium 73mg; Carbs 49.6g; Fiber 8g; Sugar 15.5g; Protein 12.8 g

Blueberry Cake

Preparation time: 18 minutes
Cooking time: 7 hours
Serves: 6

Ingredients
- 1 tbsp grapeseed oil
- ¾ cup spelt flour
- ¾ cup teff flour
- ¼ teaspoon sea salt
- 1 cup coconut milk
- ⅓ cup agave
- ½ cup fresh blueberries

Instructions:
1. Grease and line a cake pan with grapeseed oil and parchment paper. Place aside. Inspect the Instant Pot to make sure the cake pan will fit. Combine the teff flour and spelt flour in a bowl.
2. Stir in the salt after adding the other ingredients. Milk and agave should be combined in a different bowl. When the dry components are thoroughly incorporated or lumps start to form, stir the wet ingredients into the dry ingredients. Blueberries should be added last.
3. Fill the cake pan with the combined batter after greasing it. Close the cover after adding it to the Instant Pot. Verify that the vent's setting is not "sealing." Set the cooking duration at 7 hours.

Nutritional Info: Calories 289; Fat 13g; Sodium 109mg; Carbs 38.8g; Fiber 6.2g; Sugar 4.8g; Protein 7.5g

Berry-Spinach Smoothies

Preparation time: 15 minutes
Cooking time: 2 minutes
Serves: 8

Ingredients
- 2 cups frozen unsweetened strawberries
- 1 cup frozen unsweetened raspberries
- 1 cup fresh blackberries or blueberries
- 1 cup fresh baby spinach leaves
- 1 cup pomegranate juice
- 3 tbsps sugar-free vanilla-flavor protein powder, soy protein powder or nonfat dry milk powder

Instructions:
1. In a blender, combine the following ingredients: pomegranate juice, pomegranate seeds, blackberries, strawberries, and raspberries. Under cover, blend until smooth. Pour into serving glasses.

Nutritional Info: Calories 80; Fat 0.5g; Sodium 8mg; Carbs 18.6g; Fiber 2.8g; Sugar 14.7g; Protein 1.8g

Mushroom-Bell Pepper Omelet

Preparation time: 15 minutes
Cooking time: 25 minutes
Serves: 4

Ingredients
- 30 tsp garbanzo bean flour (chickpea flour)
- 2 cups water
- Sea salt, to taste
- freshly ground black pepper, to taste
- ½ cup unsweetened almond milk
- ½ of an onion, chopped
- ¼ cup fresh mushrooms, cut into slices
- ¼ cup red bell pepper, seeded and diced
- 1 tbsp chives, minced

Instructions:
1. Preheat the oven to 350°F. Grease a pie pan very lightly.
2. In a bowl, add the flour, water, salt, pepper, and almond milk. beat it until thoroughly blended.
3.0 In another bowl, combine the mushrooms, bell pepper, and onion. Evenly distribute the veggie mixture on top. Sprinkle with chives evenly. For 20 to 25 minutes, bake.
4. Slice into equal-sized slices using a knife, then serve.

Nutritional Info: Calories 149; Fat 2.33g; Sodium 134mg; Carbs 26.23g; Fiber 4.5g; Sugar 8.4g; Protein 7g

Clam and Vegetable Chowder

Preparation time: 5 minutes
Cooking time: 40 minutes
Serves: 6 to 8

Ingredients
- 1 ½ cups cooked garbanzo beans
- 1 ½ cups chopped oyster mushrooms
- 2 cups garbanzo bean flour
- 1 cup mashed white onions
- ½ cup chopped butternut squash
- ½ cup medium diced kale
- 1 cup homemade hempseed milk
- 1 cup aquafaba
- 2 tsp dill
- ½ teaspoon cayenne powder
- 2 tsp basil
- 1 tbsp pure sea salt
- 1 tbsp grapeseed oil
- 7 cups spring water

Instructions:
1. In a large pot, combine 6 cups of spring water and aquafaba.
2. Add half of each seasoning to the saucepan along with the cooked garbanzo beans, diced veggies, and beans. 3.
3. After that, combine them, bring them to a boil, and simmer for 10 minutes at medium heat, stirring occasionally.
4. In another bowl, combine the hempseed milk, grapeseed oil, 1 cup of spring water, and the remaining seasonings.
5. Gradually whisk in the chickpea flour.
6. Continue adding the flour and whisking continually until the mixture is completely smooth and lump free. Before adding it gradually to the saucepan of veggies, whisk the mixture to prevent lumps. Cook the chopped oyster mushrooms for 10 minutes over low heat. Sometimes I stir the soup. Eat some! Your vegan clam chowder is ready!

Nutritional Info: Calories 339; Fat 7g; Sodium 431mg; Carbs 53g; Fiber 11g; Sugar 12g; Protein 17.5g

Awesome White Sandwich Bread

Preparation time: 9 minutes
Cooking time: 50 minutes
Serves: 16

Ingredients
- 1 cup warm water
- 2 tbsps active dry yeast
- 4 tbsps oil
- 2 ½ tsp salt
- 2 tbsps raw sugar or 4 tbsps maple syrup/agave nectar
- 1 cup warm almond milk or any other non-dairy milk of your choice
- 6 cups all-purpose flour

Instructions:
1. In a mixing bowl, combine the yeast, sugar, and warm water. Good stirring for 5 minutes or till a little foam is required for setting.
2. Combine the flour and salt in a large mixing bowl. Good stirring
3. Combine the milk, oil, and yeast mixture into a dough. 4. Each time you need to add water to make a smooth, non-sticky dough, do it slowly and thoroughly. or, as necessary, add extra flour.
4. Using your hands or a mixer, knead the dough until it is soft and malleable.
5. Lightly mist the dough with water.
6. Place the dough in a bowl. It should be covered with a towel and left until it doubles in size.
7. Next, place the dough on a spotless, level surface. Roll out the dough.
8. Use parchment paper to line a loaf pan. If you'd rather, lubricate with some oil. Put it in a loaf pan.
9. Spray the dough with extra water, then cover it with a towel once more. Wait until the dough has doubled in bulk.
10. Preheat the oven to 370°F and bake for 40 to 50 minutes.
11. After cooling, slice into 16 equal pieces, and use as needed. Store it at room temperature in a breadbox.

Nutritional Info: Calories 226; Fat 4g; Sodium 195mg; Carbs 41g; Fiber 1.7g; Sugar 4.5g; Protein 5.6g

Avocado Blueberry Smoothie

Preparation time: 5 minutes
Cooking time: 0 minutes
Servings: 2

Ingredients:
- 1 cup crushed ice, divided
- ½ cup blueberries
- ¾ cup unsweetened almond milk
- 2 tbsps heavy (whipping) cream
- 1 tbsp coconut oil
- 1 avocado, peeled and pitted

Instructions:
1. In a blender, combine ½ cup of frosting, blueberries, almond milk, heavy cream, and coconut oil.
2. Add the avocado and the last ½ cup of icing. Blend for one minute, or until it's smooth, then serve.

Nutritional Info: Calories: 325 Kcal; Fat: 54 g; Carbs: 1 g; Protein: 1 g

Make-Ahead Smoothie

Preparation time: 10 minutes
Cooking time: 2 minutes
Serves: 5

Ingredients
- 2 ½ cups whole strawberries, blueberries, raspberries, or chopped mango, divided
- 2 ½ cups sliced banana, divided
- 5 cups unsweetened vanilla almond milk or soymilk, divided

Instructions:
1. Place ½ cup strawberries (or other fruit) and ½ cup banana in a sealable plastic sandwich bag. Repeat to create four more bags with the leftover fruit. Keep it in the freezer until you're ready to use it.
2. Add the contents of one bag and one cup of almond (or soy) milk to a blender. 3. Blend thoroughly.

Nutritional Info: Calories 163; Fat 2.3g; Sodium 118mg; Carbs 31g; Fiber 4g; Sugar 19g; Protein 7g

Low-Carb Blueberry Smoothie

Preparation time: 5 minutes
Cooking time: None
Serves: 3

Ingredients
- 14 ounces canned unsweetened coconut milk
- ½ cup unsweetened almond milk
- ½ cup blueberries (fresh or frozen)
- 4 tablespoons pea protein powder
- ½ teaspoon vanilla extract

Instructions:
1. Fill a high-speed blender with the blueberries, almond milk, pea protein powder, and vanilla.
2. Gradually add the coconut milk to achieve the desired consistency of the smoothie.
3. Blend on high until all of the ingredients are well combined and the smoothie is a light purple color.
4. You can keep your baby in the refrigerator for three to four days in a sealed container.

Nutritional Info: Calories 320; Fat 29.5g; Sodium 37mg; Carbs 11.4g; Fiber 2g; Sugar 5g; Protein 7.4g

Scrambled Tofu and Veggies

Preparation time: 15 minutes
Cooking time: 15 minutes
Serves: 2

Ingredients
- ½ tbsp olive oil
- 1 small onion, chopped finely
- 1 small red bell pepper, chopped finely
- 1 cup cherry tomatoes, chopped finely
- 1½ cups firm tofu, crumbled and chopped
- Pinch of cayenne pepper
- Pinch of ground turmeric
- Sea salt, to taste

Instructions:
1. Set a skillet on the stovetop and adjust the heat to medium. First, warm up the oil.
2. After that, sauté the bell pepper and onion for about 4 minutes.
3. Put the cherry tomatoes, chopped, into the skillet. After that, cook for 1-2 minutes.
4. Cook the tofu for 6 to 8 minutes after adding the spices (turmeric, cayenne, and salt).
5. Apply heat.

Nutritional Info: Calories 378; Fat 20.3g; Sodium 147mg; Carbs 25.4g; Fiber 7.4g; Sugar 12.4g; Protein 31.7g

Awesome Sweet Potato Salad

Preparation time: 15 to 30 minutes
Cooking time: 20 minutes
Serves: 2

For the sweet potatoes:
- 2 small sweet potato
- 1 pinch salt and pepper
- 1 tbsp coconut oil

For the Dressing:
- 3 tbsps lemon juice
- 1 pinch salt
- 1 pinch pepper
- 1 tbsp extra-virgin olive oil

For the Salad:
- 4 cups mixed greens

For Servings:
- 4 tbsps hummus
- 1 cup raw blueberries
- 1 medium ripe avocado
- Fresh chopped parsley
- 2 tbsps hemp seeds

Instructions:
1. Place a large skillet over low heat. Sweet potatoes should be added after being seasoned with salt, pepper, and coconut oil. Cook sweet potatoes till they get brown.
2. Combine lemon juice, salt, and pepper in a bowl. The serving components should be combined with the mixed greens and sweet potatoes. Mix well, dress, and serve.

Nutritional Info: Calories 458; Fat 29.3g; Sodium 662mg; Carbs 49g; Fiber 14g; Sugar 16g; Protein 8.6g

Gingered Zucchini Bacon

Preparation time: 8 minutes plus 5 hours for marinating
Cooking time: 6 minutes
Serves: 4

Ingredients
- 3 zucchinis, sliced thinly lengthwise or into large strips
- ¼ cup date sugar
- ¼ cup spring water
- 1 tbsp sea salt
- 1 tbsp onion powder
- ½ teaspoon cayenne pepper powder
- ½ teaspoon ground ginger
- 1 tbsp liquid smoke
- Grapeseed oil for frying

Instructions:
1. In a bowl, combine all the ingredients minus the grapeseed oil. Let the zucchini strips marinade for at least two hours in the refrigerator.
2. On your Instant Pot, turn the Sauté setting to high and heat the oil until it begins to slightly smoke. Fry the marinated zucchini strips until crisp, about 3 minutes per side.

Nutritional Info: Calories 72; Fat 3g; Sodium 54mg; Carbs 10.6g; Fiber 2g; Sugar 7g; Protein 2.3g

Avocado Tomato Pasta

Preparation time: 5 minutes
Cooking time: 20 minutes
Serves: 4

Ingredients
- 4 cups cooked spelt pasta
- 1 medium diced avocado
- 2 cups halved cherry tomatoes
- 1 minced fresh basil
- 1 teaspoon agave syrup
- 1 tbsp key lime juice
- ¼ cup olive oil

Instructions:
1. Put the cooked pasta in the appropriate bowl.
2. Include chopped basil, cherry tomatoes, and diced avocado in the bowl. All the components should be thoroughly mixed.
3. In another bowl, combine the key lime juice, agave syrup, olive oil, and pure sea salt.
4. Pour the liquid that has been whisked over the pasta and combine thoroughly. Please! Spaghetti with basil and avocado, please!

Nutritional Info: Calories 465; Fat 23g; Sodium 17mg; Carbs 60g; Fiber 11.8g; Sugar 8g; Protein 12g

Carrot Cantaloupe Smoothie Bowl

Preparation time: 15 minutes
Cooking time: 2 minutes
Serves: 6

Ingredients
- 4 cups frozen cubed cantaloupe (½-inch pieces)
- ¾ cup carrot juice
- Pinch of salt
- Melon balls, berries, nuts, or fresh basil for garnish

Instructions:
1. In a food processor or high-speed blender, combine cantaloupe, juice, and salt. Alternate between pulsing and blending for one to two minutes, pausing occasionally to stir and scrape the sides as necessary to keep the mixture thick and smooth.
2. Before serving, top the smoothie with additional melon, berries, almonds, or basil if desired.

Nutritional Info: Calories 289; Fat 1.5g; Sodium 994mg; Carbs 68.7g; Fiber 7g; Sugar 57g; Protein 7g

Blueberry Multigrain Pancakes

Preparation time: 5 minutes
Cooking time: 20 minutes
Servings: 6

Ingredients:
- Whole-wheat flour: ¾ cup
- All-purpose flour: 1 cup
- Rolled oats: ⅓ cup
- Stevia: 2 tbsp.
- Baking powder: 2 tsp.
- Buttermilk: 1 & ¾ cup
- Yellow cornmeal: ⅓ cup
- Unsalted plant butter: ¼ cup
- Baking soda: half tsp.
- Fresh blueberries: 1 cup
- Nutmeg: half tsp.
- Honey: ⅓ cup
- 3 eggs

Instructions:
1. Combine all of the dry ingredients in a large bowl.
2. Combine the wet ingredients, then fold in the blueberries.
3. Spray some oil on a medium flame and place it there.
4. Add the batter (¼ cup) and heat it untouched until bubbles appear.
5. Flip over and cook until golden. Serve

Nutritional Info: Calories 250 kcal; Fat 17.2 g; Carbs 76 g; Protein 6.4 g

Triple Berry Smoothie

Preparation time: 5 minutes
Cooking time: 0 minutes
Servings: 2

Ingredients:
- 1 cup crushed ice, divided
- ½ cup unsweetened almond milk
- 1 tbsp coconut oil
- ½ cup blueberries
- ½ cup raspberries
- ½ cup blackberries
- ½ tsp pure vanilla extract

Instructions:
1. In a blender, combine ½ cup of ice, almond milk, and coconut oil.
2. Stir in the remaining ½ cup icing, blueberries, raspberries, blackberries, and vanilla extract. Blend for one minute, or until it's smooth, then serve.

Nutritional Info: Calories: 290 Kcal; Fat: 22 g; Carbs: 10 g; Protein: 3 g

Bagels Made Healthy

Preparation time: 5 minutes
Cooking time: 40 minutes
Servings: 8

Ingredients:
- 1 ½ cup warm water
- 1 ¼ cup bread flour
- 2 tbsp. honey
- 2 cup whole wheat flour
- 2 tsp. yeast
- 1 ½ tbsp. olive oil
- 1 tbsp. vinegar

Instructions:
1. In a mixing machine, combine all ingredients before selecting the dough cycle.
2. Cut out eight pieces in the shape of a flattened ball.
3. Use your thumb to make a hole in the center, then construct a donut-shaped hole.
4. Place the dough in the shape of donuts on a greased baking sheet, cover it, and let it rise for about half an hour.
5. In a large saucepan, bring about 2 inches of water to a boil.
6. Cook the bagels one at a time in hot water for one minute before flipping them over.
7. Take them out and place them back on the baking sheet. Bake at 350°F for 20 to 25 minutes, or until golden brown.

Nutritional Info: Calories: 228.1 kcal; Fat: 3.7 g; Carbs: 41.8 g; Protein: 6.9 g

Simple Lime Watercress Salad

Preparation time: 5 minutes
Cooking time: 5 minutes
Serves: 2

Ingredients
- 2 cups torn watercress
- ½ cucumber, sliced
- 1 tbsp key lime juice
- 2 tbsps olive oil
- pure sea salt, to taste
- cayenne powder, to taste

Instructions:
1. Place olive oil and key lime juice in a salad bowl. Then, thoroughly blend them.
2. Slice the cucumber and add all of the slices to the bowl. 3. Add watercress to the bowl after tearing it up.
3. Season with salt and cayenne pepper to taste, then top with pure sea salt. . Enjoy your detox fast salad!

Nutritional Info: Calories 125; Fat 13.5g; Sodium 14mg; Carbs 1g; Fiber 0.2g; Sugar 0.2g; Protein 0.8g

Zucchini-Banana Bread Pancakes

Preparation time: 10 minutes
Cooking time: 40 minutes
Serves: 4

Ingredients
- 1 cup minced zucchini
- 2 cups spelt flour
- ¼ cup pureed burro bananas
- ½ cup chopped walnuts
- 2 tbsps date sugar
- 1 tbsp grapeseed oil
- 2 cups homemade walnut milk

Instructions:
1. Place the spelt flour and date sugar in a sizable bowl. Stir everything thoroughly. Put homemade walnut milk and pureed burro bananas in the bowl. Stir the ingredients together thoroughly to avoid lumps.
2. Combine the remaining ingredients in a mixing bowl with the chopped walnuts and minced zucchini. On medium heat, warm a skillet pan with grapeseed oil. To make the pancakes, pour some prepared zucchini batter into the pan (3 to 4 inches across). For each side of the pancakes, cook them for around 5 minutes.

Nutritional Info: Calories 348; Fat 16.6g; Sodium 62mg; Carbs 29g; Fiber 8g; Sugar 14.6g; Protein 26g

Apple Pumpkin Smoothie

Preparation time: 15 minutes
Cooking time: 5 minutes
Serves: 4

Ingredients
- 1 ½ cups unsweetened vanilla almond milk
- 1 ⅓ cups chopped apples (2 medium)
- ½ (15-ounce) can pumpkin
- ¾ cup plain nonfat Greek yogurt
- ½ cup ice
- 2 tbsps maple syrup
- ¼ teaspoon pumpkin pie spice
- ⅛ teaspoon salt
- ¼ cup high-protein honey-almond-flavor granola, such as Bear Naked brand

Instructions:
1. Blend almond milk, almonds, pumpkin, yogurt, ice, maple syrup, pumpkin pie spice, and salt in a blender. Cover and combine until smooth.
2. Sprinkle 1 spoonful of the granola on top of each serving.

Nutritional Info: Calories 209; Fat 6.4g; Sodium 203mg; Carbs 35g; Fiber 2g; Sugar 26g; Protein 5g

Orange-Carrot Smoothie

Preparation time: 15 minutes
Cooking time: 20 minutes
Serves: 2

Ingredients
- 1 cup sliced carrots
- ½ teaspoon finely shredded orange peel
- 1 cup orange juice
- 1 ½ cups ice cubes
- 3 (1 inch) pieces orange peel curls

Instructions:
1. Cook the carrots in a small amount of boiling water for about 15 minutes, or until very tender, in a covered small saucepan.Good drainage is cool.
2. Put the drained carrots in the blender. Add freshly squeezed orange juice and orange peel. Blend until smooth, covered. Include the ice cubes, cover, and blend until smooth. Pour into glasses. Begin with orange peel curls if desired.

Nutritional Info: Calories 167; Fat 0.8g; Sodium 87mg; Carbs 39g; Fiber 4.5g; Sugar 26.6g; Protein 3g

Vegan Chocolate Smoothie

Preparation time: 10 minutes
Cooking time: None
Serves: 1

Ingredients
- ½ ripe avocado
- 3 tablespoons cocoa powder
- 1 cup full-fat coconut milk
- ½ cup water
- 1 teaspoon lime juice
- pinch mineral salt
- 6-7 drops liquid Stevia
- Fresh mint (for decoration)

Instructions:
1. Place all the ingredients in a blender.
2. Puree on high until smooth and creamy.Add more liquid stevia, if desired, to taste.
3. If desired, garnish with fresh mint and serve.

Nutritional Info: Calories 748; Fat 72.7g; Sodium 859mg; Carbs 31g; Fiber 13.7g; Sugar 9g; Protein 8.6g

Berry-Banana Smoothie with Almonds

Preparation time: 4 minutes
Cooking time: 20 minutes
Serves: 4

Ingredients
- ⅔ cup frozen raspberries
- ½ cup frozen sliced banana
- ½ cup plain unsweetened almond milk
- 5 tablespoons sliced almonds, divided
- ¼ teaspoon ground cinnamon
- ⅛ teaspoon ground cardamom
- ⅛ teaspoon vanilla extract
- ¼ cup blueberries
- 1 tbsp unsweetened coconut flakes

Instructions:
1. In a blender, combine the following ingredients: pomegranate juice, pomegranate seeds, blackberries, strawberries, and raspberries. Unde1. In a blender, combine raspberries, banana, almond milk, 3 tbsps of almonds, cinnamon, cardamom, and vanilla and process until extremely smooth.
2. Place the smoothed mixture in a bowl and top with the remaining 2 tbsps of almonds, coconut, and blueberries. Cover and blend until smooth.Pour into serving glasses.1. In a blender, combine raspberries, banana, almond milk, 3 tbsps of almonds, cinnamon, cardamom, and vanilla and process until extremely smooth.
3. Place the smoothed mixture in a bowl and top with the remaining 2 tbsps of almonds, coconut, and blueberries.

Nutritional Info: Calories 129; Fat 2.6g; Sodium 44mg; Carbs 25.7g; Fiber 3g; Sugar 19.4g; Protein 2.6g

Almond Butter Chocolate Shake

Preparation time: 8 minutes
Cooking time: None
Serves: 1

Ingredients
- 1 ½ cup full fat coconut milk or substitute half and half
- 2 tbsps almond butter
- 2 tablespoons cocoa powder
- 1 ½ tablespoons monk fruit sweetener or more, depending on taste
- ½ teaspoon vanilla extract

Instructions:
1. Fill your blender with all the ingredients. 2. Cover your face and raise your head. Mix until thoroughly combined.
2. Try it right away, and if you think it needs a little more sweetness, add another 14 tsp of monk fruit sweetener at a time until it's just right.

Nutritional Info: Calories 236; Fat 20g; Sodium 17mg; Carbs 11g; Fiber 4.8g; Sugar 2g; Protein 7.6g

Banana-Peanut Butter

Preparation time: 5 minutes
Cooking time: 0 minutes
Servings: 1

Ingredients:
- 1 cup chopped and packed Romaine lettuce
- 1 frozen medium banana
- 1 tbsp. all-natural peanut butter
- 1 cup cold almond milk

Instructions:
1. Combine all of the ingredients in a high-powered blender.
2. Puree until smooth and creamy.
3. Provide and have fun.

Nutritional Info: Calories: 349.3 Kcal; Fat: 9.7 g; Carbs: 57.4 g; Protein: 8.1 g

Honey Green Tea Smoothie

Preparation time: 4 minutes
Cooking time: 2 minutes
Serves: 3

Ingredients
- 2 cups frozen unsweetened mixed fruit, preferably peaches and pineapple
- 1 cup cold unsweetened green tea
- 1 tbsp honey
- 1 tablespoon lemon juice

Instructions:
1. In a blender, combine the fruit, tea, honey, and lemon juice. Blend until smooth and foamy. Serve immediately.

Nutritional Info: Calories 151; Fat 0.2g; Sodium 11mg; Carbs 41g; Fiber 2.3g; Sugar 38g; Protein 0.8g

Protein Mango Smoothie

Preparation time: 10 minutes
Cooking time: 0 minutes
Servings: 1

Ingredients:
- 4 cubes ice
- ½ mango chopped
- ½ cup almond milk
- ½ cup low-fat vanilla yogurt
- 1 scoop vanilla whey protein powder

Instructions:
1. In a blender, combine the ice, mango, almond milk, yogurt, and protein powder and process until smooth.

Nutritional Info: Calories 401 kcal; Protein 44.6 g; Carbohydrates 48.7 g; Fat 4.4 g

Cauliflower-Melon Smoothies

Preparation time: 8 minutes
Cooking time: 15 minutes
Serves: 2

Ingredients
- 1 cup coarsely chopped fresh cauliflower
- 2 cups honeydew melon, cut into 1-inch cubes
- 2 cups cucumber, cut into 1-inch pieces
- ½ cup lightly packed fresh mint leaves
- ¼ cup water
- 2 tablespoons honey
- 1 cup ice cubes

Instructions:
1. Cook cauliflower for 10 to 12 minutes, or until very tender, in a small saucepan with enough boiling water to cover it. Drain. Drain and rinse with cold water to quickly cool.
2. Add the following ingredients to a blender in that order: honeydew melon, cauliflower, cumin, mint, water, and honey. Cover and blend until extremely smooth, stopping and scraping the blender's sides as necessary. Add ice cubes. Blend until smooth, covered. Pour into glasses and serve right away.
3. Locate a vertical freezer container. Cover to freeze for up to six months.
4. Thaw frozen smoothies in the fridge before serving. Well-stirred before serving.

Nutritional Info: Calories 112; Fat 1g; Sodium 47mg; Carbs 25.5g; Fiber 4.3g; Sugar 21g; Protein 3.3g

Savory Tomato-Bean Soup

Preparation time: 15 minutes
Cooking time: 1 hour 20 minutes
Serves: 6 to 8

Ingredients
- 10 chopped plum tomatoes
- 1 chopped tomatillo
- 3 cups cooked garbanzo beans
- ½ cup chopped red bell pepper
- ½ cup minced onions
- ½ cup chopped green bell pepper
- 2 tsp onion powder
- 1 teaspoon cayenne powder
- 1 teaspoon sweet basil
- 1 teaspoon oregano
- ½ teaspoon achiote
- 2 tsp pure sea salt
- 2 tsp grapeseed oil
- spring water, to cook
- sausage, for serving

Instructions:
1. In a big pot, combine the bell pepper, grapeseed oil, onions, and tomatillo. Cook vegetables for 4 to 5 minutes over medium heat.
2. Add the Garbanzo beans, spices, tomatoes, and spring water to the stockpot. Stir and cook until boiling. For about an hour, simmer the tomato-bean mixture. sometimes stir. Sliced sausage links could be added a few minutes before the soup is done cooking if desired. Serve the soup and savor it!

Nutritional Info: Calories 87; Fat 1.6g; Sodium 217mg; Carbs 18.8g; Fiber 2.4g; Sugar 14.5g; Protein 1.4g

Banana Breakfast Shake

Preparation time: 5 minutes
Cooking time: 2 minutes
Serves: 2

Ingredients
- 3 tbsps raw cacao powder
- 1 cup almond milk
- 2 frozen bananas
- 3 tbsps natural peanut butter

Instructions:
1. Fill a powerful blender with each of the items listed.
2. Blend everything together until it forms a smooth shake. 3. To get your day started, indulge in a hearty shake.

Nutritional Info: Calories 330; Fat 15g; Sodium 241mg; Carbs 41g; Fiber 9.6g; Sugar 37g; Protein 12g

Ulli's Granola

Preparation time: 10 minutes
Cooking time: 40 minutes
Servings: 26

Ingredients:
- Cashews, almonds, pumpkin seeds, dried cranberries, raisins, sunflower seeds & walnuts: 2 cups each
- Coconut flakes: 3 cups, unsweetened
- Maple syrup: half cup
- Rolled oats: 4 cups
- Canola oil: ¼ cup
- Orange oil: ⅓ cup

Instructions:
1. Preheat the oven to 300 degrees Fahrenheit.
2. Add oats, coconut flakes, almonds, and seeds to a bowl. Mix well.
3. Place the other ingredients (apart from the raisins and the cranberries) in a bowl and stir well. Mix after pouring over the dry mixture.
4. Generously spray oil onto a baking sheet and spread the mixture over it.
5. Bake for 35 to 40 minutes, rotating the dish halfway.
6. Allow to cool before adding the raisins and cranberries.
7. Serve immediately and store in the refrigerator.

Nutritional Info: Calories 190 kcal; Fat 9 g; Carbs 14.8 g; Protein 21 g

Whey Berry Spinach Chia Smoothie

Preparation time: 5 minutes
Cooking time: 0 minutes
Servings: 1

Ingredients:
- ½ cup berries (you can mix blueberries with blackberry or strawberries)
- ½ cup almond milk
- ½ scoop whey protein
- ¼ cup spinach leaves
- ½ tbsp. chia seeds

Instructions:
1. Wash all of the fruits and vegetables thoroughly. Combine the fruits and vegetables in a blender.
2. Fill the glass halfway with the mixture and take a sip.

Nutritional Info: Calories: 275 kcal; Fat: 4 g; Carbs: 29 g; Protein: 24 g

Cantaloupe-Amaranth Smoothie

Preparation time: 10 minutes
Cooking time: 0 minutes
Servings: 1

Ingredients:
- ½ Cup Cubed Cantaloupe
- ¼ Handful Green Amaranth
- ½ Cup Hemp Milk
- 1 Cup Coconut Water
- 1 Tsp Agave Syrup (if you like)

Instructions:
1. All of the items must be rinsed with clean water.
2. Slice green mango, cube canned peaches, add everything to a blender, and blend until a homogeneous smoothie is obtained.
3. Pour into a clean cup; add home-made hemp milk and maple syrup.
4. Mix them together and then drink them.

Nutritional Info: Calories: 55 kcal; Fat: 0 g; Carbs: 8 g; Protein: 1 g

Raisins-Plume Smoothie

Preparation time: 10 minutes
Cooking time: 0 minutes
Servings: 1

Ingredients:
- 1 Tsp Raisins
- 2 Sweet Cherry
- 1 Skinned Black Plume
- ¼ Coconut Water

Instructions:
1. Soak 1 teaspoon raisins in warm water for 5 seconds, then drain completely.
2. Rinse and cube the skinned black plum and sweet cherry.
Place all the ingredients into a blender and blend until a homogeneous smoothie is obtained.
4. You are now free to enjoy the inevitable detox smoothie.

Nutritional Info: Calories: 150 kcal; Fat: 1.2 g; Carbs: 79 g; Protein: 3.1 g

Apple-Banana Smoothie

Preparation time: 10 minutes
Cooking time: 0 minutes
Servings: 1

Ingredients:
- I Cup Cubed Apple
- ½ Burro Banana
- ½ Cup Cubed Mango
- ½ Cup Cubed Watermelon
- ½ Tsp Powdered Onion
- 3 Tbsp Key Lime Juice
- Date 1 tbsp rice malt syrup to Taste (If you like)

Instructions:
1. Rinse the vegetables in a clean dish of water.
2. In a blender, combine the banana, peach, mango, water, and other ingredients to make homogeneous smoothies.
3. Hand over your delicious medical detox.
4. If powdered onion is not an option, you may instead add one tbsp of finely diced raw red onion.

Nutritional Info: Calories: 99 kcal; Fat: 0.3 g; Carbs: 23 g; Protein: 1.1 g

Avocado Spinach Smoothie

Preparation time: 5 minutes
Cooking time: 0 minutes
Servings: 3-4

Ingredients:
- 1 cup spinach
- 2 avocados, peeled and seeds removed
- 1 lime, peeled
- 1 cup purified water

Instructions:
1. In a blender, combine the spinach, avocado, lime, and ½ cup of water. Blend until everything is well combined.
2. Continue blending while adding more water until you achieve the desired texture.

Nutritional Info: Calories: 288 kcal; Fat: 15 g; Carbs: 13 g; Protein: 8 g

Healthy Breakfast Sandwich

Preparation time: 5 minutes
Cooking time: 5 minutes
Servings: 2

Ingredients:
- 2 split whole-wheat English muffins
- ¾ cup of liquid egg whites
- 2 slices of fresh tomato
- ½ cup of spinach leaves

Instructions:
1. In a nonstick skillet over a medium flame, cook the egg whites until opaque, about four minutes.
2. delectable English muffins Divide the cooked egg whites between the bottoms of two muffins. Add some spinach, muffin tops, and a slice of tomato on the top.

Nutritional Info: Calories 186 kcal; Fat 1.5g; Carbohydrates 28.8 g; Protein 16.3 g

Zucchini Bread

Preparation time: 35 minutes
Cooking time: 30 minutes
Servings: 18

Ingredients:
- Canola oil: ¼ cup
- Sugar substitute: half cup
- 6 egg whites
- Vanilla extract: 2 tsp.
- All-purpose flour: 1 ¼ cups
- Baking powder: 1 tsp.
- Baking soda: 1 tsp.
- Cinnamon: 3 tsp.
- Crushed pineapple: 1 ½ cups, unsweetened
- Whole-wheat flour: 1 ¼ cups
- Shredded zucchini: 2 cups
- Applesauce: half cup, unsweetened
- Chopped walnuts: half cup

Instructions:
1. Preheat the oven to 350 degrees. Two loaf pans (9 by 5) should be oil-spattered.
2. Add vanilla, egg whites, apricot preserves, canola oil, and salt to a bowl. electric mixer and whisking till foamy and thick.
3.0 Place all the flour in a bowl and set the half cup to the side.
4. Combine the flour, powder, baking soda, and cinnamon.
5. Combine dry and liquid ingredients with an electric mixer. Blend well.
6. Add the zucchini, walnuts, and pineapple. Add the half cup of flour gradually; do not add it all at once. It ought not to be runny.
7. Add half the batter to a single pan, and bake for 50 minutes.
8. Allow to cool in the pan for ten minutes. Slice and serve.

Nutritional Info: Calories 141 kcal; Fat 5 g; Carbs 22 g; Protein 4 g

Strawberry-Orange Smoothies

Preparation time: 10 minutes
Cooking time: 0 minutes
Servings: 1

Ingredients:
- 1 Cup Diced Strawberries
- 1 Removed Back of Seville Orange
- ¼ Cup Cubed Cucumber
- ¼ Cup Romaine Lettuce
- ½ Kelp
- ½ Burro Banana
- 1 Cup Soft Jelly Coconut Water
- ½ Cup Water
- Date Sugar.

Instructions:
1. Rinse all the vegetables in clean water and place them in a clean dish.
2. Chop Romaine lettuce; slice cucumber, banana, and strawberry; peel and quarter the Seville orange.
3. Place all the ingredients into a clean blender and blend until a homogeneous smoothie is obtained.
4. Transfer the contents to a clean, large cup and strengthen your body with a palatable detox.

Nutritional Info: Calories: 298 kcal; Fat: 1 g; Carbs: 68 g; Protein: 1 g

Ginger-Pear Smoothie

Preparation time: 10 minutes
Cooking time: 0 minutes
Servings: 1

Ingredients:
- 1 Big Pear with Seed and Cured
- ½ Avocado
- ¼ Handful Watercress
- ½ Sour Orange
- ½ Cup Ginger Tea
- ½ Cup Coconut Water
- ¼ Cup Spring Water
- Date Agave Syrup to satisfaction

Instructions:
1. Boil 1 cup of ginger tea first, then cover the cup and let it cool to room temperature.
2. In a clean blender, combine all of the ingredients and blend until smooth.
3. You just made yourself a delicious detox romaine smoothie.

Nutritional Info: Calories: 101 kcal; Fat: 0 g; Carbs: 27 g; Protein: 1 g

Mango And Cucumber Smoothie

Preparation time: 5 minutes
Cooking time: 0 minutes
Servings: 2

Ingredients:
- ½ cup crushed ice or 3-4 ice cubes
- 1 cup coconut milk
- 1 mango, peeled and diced
- 1 small cucumber, peeled and chopped
- 1-2 dates, pitted
- 1 tbsp chia seeds

Instructions:
1. In a high-speed blender, combine all the ingredients and blend until smooth.
2. Serve and have fun!

Nutritional Info: Calories: 320 kcal; Fat: 2 g; Carbs: 44 g; Protein: 30g

Cereal With Cranberry-Orange Twist

Preparation time: 5 minutes
Cooking time: 0 minutes
Servings: 1

Ingredients:
- ½ cup water
- ½ cup orange juice
- ½ cup oat bran
- ¼ cup dried cranberries
- 1 cup Sugar
- ½ cup Milk

Instructions:
1. Mix all ingredients together in a bowl.
2. Microwave the bowl for 2 minutes before serving with milk and sugar.
3. Enjoy!

Nutritional Info: Calories: 220.4 kcal; Fat: 2.4 g; Carbs: 43.5 g; Protein: 6.2 g

Whole-Wheat Pretzels

Preparation time: 80 minutes
Cooking time: 30 minutes
Servings: 14

Ingredients:
- Brown sugar: 2 tsp.
- Kosher salt: half tsp.
- Active dry yeast: 1 pack
- Whole-wheat flour: 3 cups
- Baking soda: ¼ cup
- 1 ½ cups of warm water
- Olive oil: 1 tbsp.
- Wheat gluten: half cup
- Sesame seeds: 1 tbsp.
- 1 egg white
- Bread flour: 1 cup

Instructions:
1. Stir in warm water, yeast, salt, and sugar in a food processor.2. Stir it and let it sit for five minutes.
2. Add the flour, oil, and glutamine.3. For five to ten minutes, or until the dough begins to pull away from the bowl, mix with a hook attachment.
3. Brush the dough and the basin with oil, cover, and bake for 60 minutes.
4. Divide it into 14 pieces. Make each part into a pretzel.
5. Fill a large saucepan halfway with water (8 to 10 cups) and 3 tbsps baking soda.Bring it to a boil.
6. Boil the pretzels for 50 seconds at a time.Take a baking sheet with a parchment paper liner and start baking.
7. Brush the boiled pretzels with egg white and sprinkle them with the same herbs.
8. Bake for 10-15 minutes at 450°F.

Nutritional Info: Calories: 148 kcal; Fat 2 g; Carbs 27 g; Protein 8 g

Nori Clove Smoothies

Preparation time: 10 minutes
Cooking time: 0 minutes
Servings: 1

Ingredients:
- ¼ Cup Fresh Nori
- 1 Cup Cubed Banana
- 1 Tsp Diced Onion or ¼ Tsp Powdered Onion
- ½ Tsp Clove
- 1 Tbsp Agave Syrup

Instructions:
1. Rinse the items in clean water.
2. Take 1 teaspoon finely chopped onion and 1 slice fresh nori.
3. Boil 1 ½ tsp in 2 cups of water, then remove the piece, cool, and measure 1 cup of tea extract.
4. Combine all the ingredients in a blender with the tea extract and blend until the smoothies are homogeneous.
5. Pour into a clean cup and enjoy some quality time with a lovely body energizer.

Nutritional Info: Calories: 78 kcal; Fat: 2.3 g; Carbs: 5 g; Protein: 6 g

Garbanzo Squash Smoothie

Preparation time: 10 minutes
Cooking time: 0 minutes
Servings: 1

Ingredients:
- 1 Large Cubed Apple
- 1 Fresh Tomatoes
- 1 Tbsp Finely Chopped Fresh Onion or ¼ Tsp Powdered Onion
- ¼ Cup Boiled Garbanzo Bean
- ½ Cup Coconut Milk
- ¼ Cubed Mexican Squash Chayote
- 1 Cup Energy Booster Tea

Instructions:
1. The items must be thoroughly rinsed with clean water.
2. Cook the garbanzo beans, then drain and cool them.
3. Place all the ingredients in a high-speed blender and blend until a homogeneous smoothie is obtained.
4. You may provide a suggested date.
5. Present your delectable smoothie and beverage.

Nutritional Info: Calories: 82 kcal; Fat: 0 g; Carbs: 22 g; Protein: 2 g

Tamarind-Pear Smoothie

Preparation time: 10 minutes
Cooking time: 0 minutes
Servings: 1

Ingredients:
- ½ Burro Banana
- ½ Cup Watermelon
- 1 Raspberries
- 1 Prickly Pear
- 1 Grape with Seed
- 3 Tamarind
- ½ Medium Cucumber
- 1 Cup Coconut Water
- ½ Cup Distilled Water

Instructions:
1. Rinse all the items with clean water.
2. Remove the tamarind pod and place the edible portion surrounding the seed in a container.
3. If you must use the seeds, boil them for 15 minutes and then add them to the tamarind-edible portion in the container.
4. Cube all the other edible fruits and transfer all the ingredients to a high-speed blender. Blend the mixture to get a homogeneous smoothie.

Nutritional Info: Calories: 199 kcal; Fat: 1 g; Carbs: 47 g; Protein: 6 g

Scrumptious Breakfast Salad

Preparation time: 35 minutes
Cooking time: 5 minutes
Servings: 4

Ingredients:
- 5 eggs
- 2 avocados, diced
- 1 chopped, head romaine lettuce
- 2 large tomatoes, diced
- 4 clementines, segmented and peeled
- 1 pint of fresh strawberries, diced
- ¼ cup of vinaigrette salad dressing
- 1 ripe mango, diced and peeled
- 1 Spanish onion, diced into rounds
- 1 Pink Lady apple, diced
- 1 cucumber, diced
- 1 nectarine, diced

Instructions:
1. In a sauté pan, crack the eggs and add the water. Once the heat has been reduced and turned off, simmer the eggs in the boiling water for ten minutes.
2. Layer lettuce, tomatoes, avocados, cucumbers, cilantro, onions, and apricots in a large mixing bowl or on separate serving plates. Vinaigrette should be poured on top.
3. Take all the eggs out of the boiling water and place them in a sink of cold running water to cool. Peel and slice the strawberries. The eggs should be placed on top of the salad.
Chef's Note
4. Remove anything you want. A further delicious addition is perfectly cut steak or salmon. Tuna or beef carpaccio performs well.
5. You may use an apple cider vinaigrette or strawbery if you'd like.

Nutritional Info: Calories: 448 kcal; Fat 24.2 g; Carbohydrates 53.7 g; Protein 13.4 g

Mediterranean Toast

Preparation time: 10 minutes
Cooking time: 0 minutes
Servings: 2

Ingredients:
- 1 ½ tsp. reduced-Fat crumbled feta
- 3 cherry tomatoes, sliced
- 3 sliced Greek olives
- 1 slice whole-wheat bread
- 1 tbsp. hummus
- ¼ avocado, mashed
- 1 egg, hardboiled

Instructions:
1. Toast the bread and then top it with 1 tbsp of hummus and ¼ of mashed avocado.
2. Add cherry tomatoes, olives, a hard-boiled egg, and feta to the salad in step two.
3. Season with salt and pepper to taste.

Nutritional Info: Calories: 333.7 kcal; Fat: 17 g; Carbs: 33.3 g; Protein: 16.3 g

Green Protein Smoothie

Preparation time: 5 minutes
Cooking time: 0 minutes
Servings: 1

Ingredients:
- 4 cubes ice
- ½ cup spinach
- ½ cup soy milk
- ⅛ cup fresh mint leaves
- 1 scoop vanilla whey protein powder
- 1 tbsp almonds

Instructions:
1. In a blender cup, combine the following ingredients: almonds, spinach, soy milk, protein powder, and icing.
2. Blend until smooth.

Nutritional Info: Calories: 282 kcal; Fat 6.5 g; Carbohydrates 13 g; Protein 43.6 g

Almond Butter Cherry Smoothie

Preparation time: 4 minutes
Cooking time: 20 minutes
Serves: 3

Ingredients
- ½ cup oat milk
- 1 tbsp almond butter
- 1 teaspoon cocoa powder
- ½ teaspoon vanilla extract
- 1 cup frozen dark sweet cherries
- 1 tablespoon brown sugar, optional

Instructions:
1. Fill a blender with the following ingredients: almond butter, chocolate, vanilla, raisins, and cumin (if using).
2. Blend thoroughly.

Nutritional Info: Calories 138; Fat 4g; Sodium 21mg; Carbs 30g; Fiber 3g; Sugar 25g; Protein 3g

Morning Smoothie

Preparation time: 15 minutes
Cooking time: 2 minutes
Serves: 4

Ingredients
- 1 ¼ cups orange juice, preferably calcium-fortified
- 1 banana
- 1 ¼ cups frozen berries, such as raspberries, blackberries, blueberries, or strawberries
- ½ cup low-fat silken tofu, or low-fat plain yogurt
- 1 tbsp sugar, or Splenda Granular (optional)

Instructions:
1. In a blender, combine orange juice, banana, strawberries, tofu (or yogurt), and sugar (or Splenda), if using. Blend until smooth, covered. Serve immediately.

Nutritional Info: Calories 166; Fat 1.3g; Sodium 18mg; Carbs 39g; Fiber 3.6g; Sugar 30.7g; Protein 2.6g

Healthy Strawberry Smoothie

Preparation time: 10 minutes
Cooking time: 0 minutes
Servings: 2

Ingredients:
- 1 banana
- 1 cup of almond milk
- 1 tbsp slivered almonds
- ½ cup strawberries, frozen
- 3 tbsp rolled oats
- ⅓ cup Greek yogurt, plain fat-free

Instructions:
1. Blend banana, almond milk, yogurt, strawberries, almonds, and oats until smooth in a blender.

Nutritional Info: Calories: 174 kcal; Fat: 3.8 g; Carbs: 30.1 g; Protein: 6.4 g

Currant Elderberry Smoothie

Preparation time: 10 minutes
Cooking time: 0 minutes
Servings: 1

Ingredients:
- ¼ Cup Cubed Elderberry
- 1 Sour Cherry
- 2 Currant
- 1 Cubed Burro Banana
- 1 Fig
- 1Cup 4 Bay Leaves Tea
- 1 Cup Energy Booster Tea
- Date Sugar to your satisfaction

Instructions:
1. Rinse everything in clean water.
2. Bring ¾ teaspoon of energy booster tea and 2 cups of water to a boil over high heat for 10 minutes.
3. Continue to boil for 4 minutes after adding 4 bay leaves.
4. Pour the tea extract into a clean, large cup and let it cool.
5. Transfer all of the ingredients into a high-speed blender, and blend until a homogeneous smoothie is obtained.
6. Pour the tasty medical smoothie into a clean cup and enjoy.

Nutritional Info: Calories: 63 kcal; Fat: 0.22 g; Carbs: 15.5 g; Protein: 1.6 g

Matcha Smoothie

Preparation time: 5 minutes
Cooking time: 0 minutes
Servings: 1

Ingredients:
- 4 cubes ice
- ¾ tsp green tea powder (matcha)
- ½ cup low-fat vanilla Greek-style yogurt
- 1 cup low-fat soy milk

Instructions:
1. Use a blender to thoroughly smash the icing before blending it with the yogurt and soy milk.

Nutritional Info: Calories: 186 kcal; Fat 2.3 g; Carbohydrates 27 g; Protein 16 g

Kale and Sweet Potato Hash

Preparation time: 10 minutes
Cooking time: 15 minutes
Serves: 2

Ingredients
- 1 teaspoon avocado oil
- 2 cups peeled and cubed sweet potatoes
- ½ cup chopped kale
- ½ cup diced onion
- ½ teaspoon sea salt
- ½ teaspoon freshly ground black pepper
- ½ avocado, cubed (optional)
- 1 to 2 tsp sesame seeds or hemp seeds (optional)

Instructions:
1. Heat the avocado oil in a large skillet over medium heat. When the sweet potatoes are tender, add the kale, onion, salt, and pepper and sauté for 10 to 15 minutes. Get rid of the heat.
2. Transfer to 1 large or 2 small dishes, and serve after gently incorporating the avocado and sesame seeds (if using).

Nutritional Info: Calories 143; Fat 10.7g; Sodium 397mg; Carbs 12g; Fiber 6.4g; Sugar 2g; Protein 2.8g

Brazil Lettuce Smoothies

Preparation time: 10 minutes
Cooking time: 0 minutes
Servings: 1

Ingredients:
- 1 Cup Raspberries
- ½ Handful Romaine Lettuce
- ½ Cup Walnut Milk
- 2 Brazil Nuts
- ½ Large Grape with Seed
- 1 Cup Soft jelly Coconut Water
- Date 1 tbsp rice malt syrup to Taste

Instructions:
1. Rinse the vegetables in a clean dish of water.
2. Chop the Romaine lettuce and strawberries, then add them to the blender and blend until the smoothies are homogeneous.
3. Hand over your delicious medical detox.

Nutritional Info: Calories: 168 kcal; Fat: 4.5 g; Carbs: 31.3 g; Protein: 3.6 g

Apple Pancakes

Preparation time: 5 minutes
Cooking time: 5 minutes
Servings: 16

Ingredients:
- ¼ cup extra-virgin olive oil and divided 1 cup whole wheat flour
- 2 tsp. baking powder 1 tsp. baking soda
- 1 tsp. ground cinnamon 1 cup 1mg milk
- 2 large eggs
- 1 medium Gala apple, diced 2 tbsp. maple syrup
- ¼ cup chopped walnuts

Instructions:
1. Set aside 1 teaspoon of oil to use for greasing a skillet or griddle.
2. In a large mixing bowl, combine the flour, baking powder, baking soda, cinnamon, whole eggs, almonds, and remaining oil.
3. Heat the reserved oil in a skillet over medium-high heat. Pour in around ¼ cup of the batter for each cake as you work in batches. Cook until both sides are browned.
4. Put four cakes into each of the medium storage containers and four small containers with the maple syrup.
5. To serve, top each serving with a sprinkle of walnuts and a drizzle of maple syrup.

Nutritional Info: Calories: 378 kcal; Fat: 22 g; Carbs: 39 g; Protein: 10 g

Muesli Scones

Preparation time: 20 minutes
Cooking time: 30 minutes
Servings: 16

Ingredients:
- Celtic sea salt: half tsp.
- Dried apricots: ¼ cup, chopped
- Baking soda: half tsp.
- Almond flour: 2 cups, blanched
- Honey: 2 tbsp.
- Dried cranberries: ¼ cup
- 1 egg
- Sesame seeds, sunflower seeds & pistachios (chopped): ¼ cup each

Instructions:
1. In a mixing bowl, combine the soda, flour, and salt. Add nuts, dried fruits, and seeds.
2. In a mixing bowl, combine the eggs and honey. Add wet ingredients to dry ones.
3. Mix everything together by hand and form a dough.
4. Make the dough ¾" thick. Cut each piece into 16 equal pieces and shape each piece into a square.
5. Bake for 10 to 12 minutes at 350°F on a baking sheet lined with parchment paper.
6. Serv.

Nutritional Info: Calories: 121 kcal; Fat 7.3 g; Carbs 18.1 g; Protein 8.2 g

Strawberry-Kiwifruit Smoothies

Preparation time: 5 minutes
Cooking time: 2 minutes
Serves: 8

Ingredients
- 4 cups sliced fresh strawberries
- 1 medium banana, sliced
- 1 (6-ounce) container vanilla low-fat yogurt
- 1 cup ice cubes
- 1 kiwifruit, peeled and sliced, optional

Instructions:
1. Combine strawberries, banana, and yogurt in a blender; cover and process until smooth. Blend until smooth while adding ice cubes one at a time through the lid's hole while the blender is running. Pour into 8 tiny glasses. Kiwifruit can be used as a garnish if desired; serve right away.

Nutritional Info: Calories 61; Fat 0.7g; Sodium 17mg; Carbs 13g; Fiber 2.4g; Sugar 8.5g; Protein 2g

Chewy Breakfast Cookies

Preparation time: 5 minutes
Cooking time: 10 minutes
Servings: 12

Ingredients:
- 1 cup gluten-free old-fashioned rolled oats
- 2 medium ripe bananas, mashed
- 1 tbsp unsalted almond butter
- tbsps chia seeds
- ½ tsp baking powder
- ¾ tsp pure vanilla extract
- ¼ tsp sea salt
- ¼ cup dark chocolate chips

Instructions:
1. Your air fryer should first be preheated to 320°F.
2. Combine the oatmeal, bananas, almond butter, chia seeds, baking powder, vanilla, and salt in a large basin. 3. Gently incorporate the chocolate chunks.
3. Drop the dough in rounded tbspfuls, one inch apart, directly into the air fryer pan, working in batches if necessary.
4. 4. Prepare the dish for 10 minutes, or until golden brown. Before serving, allow some cooling.

Nutritional Info: Calories: 260 kcal; Fat: 10g; Carbs: 38 g; Protein: 6 g

Spinach-Grapefruit Smoothie

Preparation time: 8 minutes
Cooking time: 2 minutes
Serves: 6

Ingredients
- 1 cup plain coconut water
- 1 cup frozen diced pineapple
- 1 cup packed baby spinach
- 1 small grapefruit, peeled and segmented, plus any juice squeezed from the membranes
- ½ teaspoon grated fresh ginger
- 1 cup ice

Instructions:
1. Blend coconut water, ginger, and salt in a blender together with the pineapple, grapefruit, and any other juices. Blend until smooth and foamy.

Nutritional Info: Calories 34; Fat 0.2g; Sodium 47mg; Carbs 8g; Fiber 1.3g; Sugar 6g; Protein 0.8g

No-Cook Overnight Oats

Preparation time: 5 minutes
Cooking time: 0 minutes
Servings: 1

Ingredients:
- 1 ½ cup low fat milk
- 5 whole almond pieces
- 1 tsp. chia seeds
- 2 tbsp. oats
- 1 tsp. sunflower seeds
- 1 tbsp. raisins

Instructions:
1. Place all of the ingredients in a jar or Mason jar with a lid.
2. Overnight refrigeration
3. Enjoy breakfast. Keep it chilled for up to three days.

Nutritional Info: Calories: 271 kcal; Fat: 9.8 g; Carbs: 35.4 g; Protein: 16.7 g

Vegan and Vegetarian Recipes

Herbed Irish Stew

Preparation time: 10 minutes
Cooking time: 15 minutes
Serves: 8

Ingredients
- ¼ cup extra-virgin olive oil
- 3 leeks, thinly sliced
- 1 cup chopped red potatoes
- 1 cup peeled and sliced parsnips
- 1 cup peeled and chopped turnip
- 1 cup sliced celery
- 1 cup sliced carrots
- 4 cups garbanzo beans, drained
- 4 cups low-sodium vegetable broth
- 2 cups vegan stout beer (such as Samuel Smith's)
- ½ cup chopped fresh parsley
- ¼ teaspoon dried rosemary
- ¼ teaspoon dried thyme
- ¼ teaspoon dried marjoram
- ¼ cup water (optional)
- salt and ground black pepper to taste

Instructions:
1. Place the right pot on the stove and turn the heat to medium-high. 2. Heat it up after adding the olive oil. Leeks should be cooked for 3 to 5 minutes, or until translucent.
2. Add potatoes, parsnips, turnips, celery, and carrots to the mix.4 minutes of cooking and stirring, or until slightly soft and covered in oil.
3. Optional ingredients include parsley, vegetable broth, garbanzo beans, and beer. The stew should boil.
4. Continue cooking the mixture for another hour or two, or until the vegetables are tender and the stew has considerably thickened. Insert the herbs. Add a splash of water if necessary; season with salt and pepper to taste.

Nutritional Info: Calories 168; Fat 2.3g; Sodium 526mg; Carbs 33g; Fiber 7g; Sugar 10g; Protein 5.9g

Brown Lentils

Preparation time: 8 minutes
Cooking time: 10 minutes
Serves: 4

Ingredients
- 1 cup brown or green lentils, rinsed well and drained
- 1 ¾ cups filtered water
- ½ teaspoon sea salt
- ¼ teaspoon black pepper

Instructions:
1. Fill a 6-quart pressure cooker halfway with rinsed lentils and water.Salt and pepper should be added.
2. Close the cover and set the timer for 10 minutes at full pressure.After the cooking is finished, let the pressure fall naturally for about 10 minutes. Use the quick release to release any leftover pressure after that.
3. Whether hot or at room temperature, serve the lentils.

Nutritional Info: Calories 169; Fat 0.5g; Sodium 294mg; Carbs 30.5g; Fiber 5.2g; Sugar 1g; Protein 11.84g

Awesome Mushroom Stroganoff

Preparation time: 10 minutes
Cooking time: 15 minutes
Serves: 1

Ingredients
- 8 ounces oyster mushrooms
- 1 tbsp oil, or to taste
- 1 small onion, diced
- 1 tbsp all-purpose flour
- 1 cup almond milk
- 1 tbsp lemon juice
- salt and ground black pepper to taste

Instructions:
1. Using a fork, shred the mushrooms.
2. Place a skillet on the stove and turn the heat to medium-high. The oil is then heated.
3. Stir in the mushrooms and onion and cook for 2 to 3 minutes, or until the vegetables are soft. While stirring, add the flour and simmer for a short while.
4. In a mixing bowl, combine almond milk and lemon juice. For 7 to 8 minutes, cook. To taste, add salt and pepper to the food.

Nutritional Info: Calories 989; Fat 19g; Sodium 206mg; Carbs 211g; Fiber 29g; Sugar 31.7g; Protein 26g

Basil-Spinach Lasagna

Preparation time: 15 minutes
Cooking time: 50 minutes
Serves: 8

Ingredients
- 2 tbsps olive oil
- 1 ½ cup chopped onion
- 3 tbsps minced garlic
- 4 (14.5 ounces) cans stewed tomatoes
- ⅓ cup tomato paste
- ½ cup chopped fresh basil
- ½ cup chopped parsley
- 1 teaspoon salt
- 1 teaspoon ground black pepper
- 1 (16 ounces) package lasagna noodles
- 2 pounds firm tofu
- 2 tbsps minced garlic
- ¼ cup chopped fresh basil
- ¼ cup chopped parsley
- ½ teaspoon salt
- ground black pepper to taste
- 3 (10 ounces) packages frozen chopped spinach, thawed and drained

To make the tomato sauce:
1. To make the sauce, get a large, heavy saucepan ready and heat the olive oil over medium heat.
2. In the pot, sauté the onions for 5 minutes, or until they are soft. Add the garlic and cook for a further five minutes.
3. In a saucepan, mix the tomatoes, tomato paste, basil, and parsley. Give the sauce a good stir, turn the heat down to low, and cover it for an hour.
4. While the sauce is simmering, bring a large saucepan of salted water to a boil. The lasagna noodles should be boiled for nine minutes, drained, and thoroughly rinsed.
5. Preheat the oven to 400 degrees Fahrenheit.
6. Combine all of the tofu blocks in a sizable mixing bowl. 7. In a mixing dish, combine the parsley, basil, and garlic. Squeeze the tofu pieces with your fingers to combine everything after adding the salt and pepper. completely combined.

To make the lasagna:
1. Spread 1 cup tomato sauce in the bottom of a 9x13-inch casserole pan. One layer of lasagna noodles should be placed, followed by one-third of the tofu mixture.
2. Evenly distribute the spinach over the tofu.
3. Add another layer of noodles on top of the tofu, then 1 and a half cups of tomato sauce.
4. Next, top the noodles with another third of the tofu mixture, add 1 ½ cups of tomato sauce, and add one more layer of noodles on top of the tomato sauce to complete the dish.
5. To finish, spoon the remaining tomato sauce over the noodles and sprinkle the remaining ⅓ of the tofu on top.
6. Bake the lasagna in the oven for 30 minutes with the foil on.
7. Serve and enjoy right away.

Nutritional Info: Calories 377; Fat 17.7g; Sodium 1043mg; Carbs 34g; Fiber 12.7g; Sugar 10.7g; Protein 30g

Chocolate Zucchini Brownies

Preparation time: 10 minutes
Cooking time: 30 minutes
Serves: 2

Ingredients
- cooking spray
- 1 cup white sugar
- ½ cup brown sugar
- ½ cup olive oil
- 1 tbsp of vanilla extract
- 2 cups all-purpose flour
- ½ cup cocoa powder (such as Hershey's®)
- 1 ½ tsp baking soda
- 1 teaspoon salt
- 3 cups shredded zucchini 1 cup vegan chocolate chips

Instructions:
1. Preheat the oven to 350 degrees Fahrenheit. Apply cooking spray to a baking pan that will work.
2. In a large mixing bowl, combine the sugar, brown sugar, and olive oil and beat with an electric mixer until well combined. Combine in the vanilla extract. Mix the flour, baking soda, salt, and cocoa powder thoroughly. (It will be a dry mixture.)
3. Using a spoon, thoroughly incorporate the zucchini into the mixture. Give the mixture five minutes to get more wet. Add the vegan chocolate chips and stir. Fill the prepared pan with the batter.
4. Bake for 25 to 30 minutes, or until the top is dry and the edges start to pull away from the pan's sides. Before cutting, let it completely cool.

Nutritional Info: Calories 1656; Fat 63g; Sodium 2161mg; Carbs 269g; Fiber 13.7g; Sugar 158g; Protein 21g

Vegan Jalapeno Poppers and Mushrooms

Preparation time: 10 minutes
Cooking time: 30 minutes
Serves: 2

Ingredients
- 1 tbsp vegetable oil
- 12 medium jalapeno peppers
- 1 (8 ounces) package button mushrooms, finely diced
- ½ cup finely diced onion
- 2 cloves garlic, minced
- 1 (8 ounces) tub vegan cream cheese substitute, softened
- 1 cup vegan shredded cheese substitute, divided
- salt and ground black pepper to taste

Instructions:
1. Remove the seeds from the pepper and cut it in half.
2. Preheat the oven to 375 degrees Fahrenheit.Place the jalapeo halves on a baking sheet covered with aluminum foil, open side up.
3. Put the vegetable oil in a pan and heat it up over medium-high heat.
4. Add the mushrooms, onion, and garlic and sauté for 8 minutes, or until the mushrooms are tender and have released their liquid. To absorb any extra liquid, move the vegetables to a dish lined with paper towels.
5. In a mixing bowl, combine the mushroom mixture, fake cream cheese, ¼ cup fake shredded cheese, salt, and pepper. On the baking sheet, spoon the mixture into the jalapeo pepper halves.
6. Bake for about 20 minutes, or until well cooked, in the oven that has been prepared.
7. Remove from the oven.
8. Sprinkle the top with the remaining ¼ cup of the cheese replacement.
9. After that, broil the dish in the hot oven for one to two minutes, or until the cheese is melted and gently browned.

Nutritional Info: Calories 865; Fat 29g; Sodium 1184mg; Carbs 137g; Fiber 16g; Sugar 48.6g; Protein 32g

Mayo Mushroom Sandwich

Preparation time: 10 minutes
Cooking time: 15 minutes
Serves: 2

Ingredients
- ½ cup vegan Worcestershire sauce
- ½ cup tamari soy sauce
- ½ cup water
- 1 shiitake mushroom
- 1 tbsp fermented black bean paste
- 1 tbsp minced shallot
- 1 clove garlic, crushed
- 1 strip nori seaweed
- 4 ½ ounces tempeh
- ¼ cup vegan mayonnaise
- 1 teaspoon sriracha sauce
- 1 (6 inches) French baguette, sliced into bite-sized cubes
- 1 tbsp olive oil
- 1 jalapeno pepper, sliced
- ½ ounce pickled daikon, or to taste
- ½ ounce pickled carrot, or to taste
- 2 cucumbers, sliced to taste
- 3 tbsps chopped fresh cilantro

Instructions:
1. Preheat the oven to 350°F with care.Next, line a baking sheet with parchment paper.
2. Heat the Worcestershire sauce, tamari, Worcestershire sauce, water, mushroom, black bean paste, shallot, garlic clove, and seaweed in a pot over medium heat.Immediately turn off the heat and let it cool down. Remove the sauce from the pan after discarding the sediments.
3. In a bowl, mix the tempeh with ⅓ cup of the sauce. Tempeh should be marinated for 20 minutes, turning it halfway through.
4. On another plate, combine 1 teaspoon of the tempeh marinade, vegan mayo, and sriracha. Keep it chilled until you're ready to use it.
5. Arrange the baguette slices on the baking sheet that has been oiled with olive oil. Place the bread in a single layer after tossing it.
6.Bake in a preheated oven for 15 minutes. About 8 minutes longer of cooking is required to brown the bread. Transfer it to a bowl for mixing.
7. Spread the liquid aside and arrange the tempeh on a baking sheet. The remaining marinade should be basted halfway through the ten minutes of baking. Continue baking for 10 more minutes, basting halfway through.
8.Cut the tempeh into cubes. Bread, tempeh, chopped jalapenos, pickled daikon, carrot, cucumber, and cilantro should be placed in serving bowls. Serve with Sriracha mayo on top.

Nutritional Info: Calories 612; Fat 27g; Sodium 6404mg; Carbs 71g; Fiber 6g; Sugar 17g; Protein 28g

Vanilla Mug Brownie

Preparation time: 10 minutes
Cooking time: 1 minutes
Serves: 1

Ingredients
- 2 tsp white sugar, or to taste
- 2 tsp unsweetened cocoa powder
- ¼ teaspoon baking soda
- 1 pinch salt
- ¼ cup water
- 2 tbsps canola oil
- ⅛ teaspoon vanilla extract
- 2 tsp vegan chocolate chips (such as Enjoy Life®)

Instructions:
1. In a cup that can be microwaved, combine whole wheat flour, white sugar, cocoa powder, baking soda, and salt. Add the canola oil, vanilla essence, and water. Add the chocolate chunks and stir.
2. Microwave for 50 to 1 minute, or until thoroughly heated.

Nutritional Info: Calories 496; Fat 35g; Sodium 793mg; Carbs 44g; Fiber 4.8g; Sugar 13g; Protein 5.8g

Chocolate Mug Cake

Preparation time: 10 minutes
Cooking time: 5 minutes
Serves: 1

Ingredients
- 4 tbsps all-purpose flour
- 3 tbsps white sugar
- 2 tbsps unsweetened cocoa powder
- ¼ teaspoon baking powder
- 4 tbsps applesauce
- 3 tbsps soy milk
- 1 tbsp vegan chocolate chips, or more to taste
- 1 tbsp toasted flaked coconut (optional)

Instructions:
1. In a cup, mash together the flour, sugar, cocoa powder, and baking powder. In another bowl, combine the soy milk and applesauce and add it to the flour mixture. To combine, thoroughly stir everything together. Add the chocolate chunks and coconut on top after folding.
2. Microwave on high for 3 minutes, or until the mug cake is properly risen and set.

Nutritional Info: Calories 460; Fat 10.8g; Sodium 168mg; Carbs 88.6g; Fiber 6g; Sugar 43g; Protein 9g

Vegan Au Gratin Potatoes

Preparation time: 10 minutes
Cooking time: 20 minutes
Serves: 6

Ingredients
- 6 large potatoes, peeled and cubed
- 1 ¼ cups vegetable broth, divided
- 2 tbsps all-purpose flour
- 1 teaspoon seasoning salt
- ½ teaspoon ground black pepper
- ¼ teaspoon dry mustard
- 1 cup soft bread crumbs
- ⅛ teaspoon nutmeg
- 2 cups soy milk
- 1 ½ cups Cheddar-flavored soy cheese, shredded and divided
- 3 tsp paprika

Instructions:
1. Preheat the oven to 350°F with care.
2. In a small mixing bowl, combine nutmeg, mustard, flour, pepper, and seasoning salt. Mix well.
3. Fill a large pot halfway with salted water. Add the potatoes after bringing all the ingredients to a boil.
4. Boil the potatoes for about 15 minutes, or until they are cooked but firm. After draining, put the food in a 9 x 13-inch baking dish.
5. In the meantime, heat up two tbsps of broth in a small pot. Reduce the heat to low.
6. In the saucepan, stir in the nutmeg-mustard combination.
7. Gradually add the soy milk, stirring constantly, until the mixture thickens. Add the soy cheese in two batches. To melt the cheese, constantly stir. apply to potatoes.
8. In a small mixing bowl, combine the bread crumbs and the remaining broth.
9. Spoon over the potatoes evenly. Add the remaining soy cheese over top. Add paprika to the mixture.
10. Bake for 20 minutes in a preheated oven.
11.

Nutritional Info: Calories 495; Fat 13g; Sodium 823mg; Carbs 76.8g; Fiber 9g; Sugar 7g; Protein 19g

Baked Vegan Pancakes

Preparation time: 10 minutes
Cooking time: 15 minutes
Serves: 1

Ingredients
- 1 ¼ cups all-purpose flour
- 2 tbsps white sugar
- 2 tsp baking powder
- ½ teaspoon salt
- 1¼ cups water
- 1 tbsp oil

Instructions:
1. In a large mixing bowl, sift together the flour, sugar, baking powder, and salt; make a well in the center.
2. In another dish, thoroughly mix the water and oil.
3. After that, pour the flour amalgam into the There will be lumps in the mixture; stir just until incorporated.
4. Heat a griddle that has been lightly oiled over medium-high heat.
5. Spoon large amounts of batter onto the griddle. Cook until bubbles form and the edges are completely dried.
6. Cook again for 1 to 2 minutes, or until the bottoms are browned. Continue by using the remaining batter.

Nutritional Info: Calories 760; Fat 15g; Sodium 1181mg; Carbs 140g; Fiber 4.4g; Sugar 16g; Protein 16g

Mayo Vegan Coleslaw

Preparation time: 10 minutes plus 2 hours for chilling
Cooking time: 15 minutes
Serves: 2

Ingredients
- 1 (16 ounces) bag coleslaw mix
- ⅔ cup vegan mayonnaise (such as Follow Your Heart® Vegenaise®)
- ½ cup granular sucralose sweetener (such as Splenda®)
- 3 tbsps olive oil
- 1 tbsp white vinegar
- 1 tbsp poppy seeds
- ¼ teaspoon salt

Instructions:
1. Place the coleslaw mix in an appropriate mixing dish and stir thoroughly. 2.
2. In a small mixing bowl, combine vegan mayonnaise, sweetener, olive oil, vinegar, poppy seeds, and salt. 3. Fold the coleslaw mixture into the dressing gradually.
3. Chill the coleslaw for at least two hours before serving. Offer cold.

Nutritional Info: Calories 521; Fat 48g; Sodium 1013mg; Carbs 16g; Fiber 6g; Sugar 3g; Protein 9g

Lemony Vanilla Cake

Preparation time: 10 minutes
Cooking time: 35 minutes
Serves: 2

Ingredients
- 1 cup plain soy milk
- 1 tbsp apple cider vinegar
- 1 ½ cups unbleached all-purpose flour
- 1 cup white sugar
- 1 teaspoon baking soda
- 1 teaspoon baking powder
- ½ teaspoon salt
- ⅓ cup canola oil
- ¼ cup water
- 1 tbsp lemon juice
- 1 tbsp vanilla extract
- ¼ teaspoon almond extract

Instructions:
1. Preheat the oven to 350°F with care. 8x8-inch greased and dusted baking dish
2. In a suitable measuring cup made of glass, combine the soy milk and vinegar.
3. In a mixing bowl, combine the sugar, baking soda, flour, baking powder, and salt.
4. With a fork, quickly blend the soy milk mixture with the canola oil, water, lemon juice, vanilla, and almond extracts. Once the batter is lump-free, add the soy milk mixture. The prepared baking dish should now be filled with the batter.
5. Bake the cake for 35 minutes or until a toothpick inserted into the center comes out clean.

Nutritional Info: Calories 935; Fat 39g; Sodium 1285mg; Carbs 130.5g; Fiber 2.6g; Sugar 56.7g; Protein 11.7g

Lemony Artichokes

Preparation time: 15 minutes
Cooking time: 23 minutes
Serves: 3

Ingredients
- 2 large artichokes
- 1 ½ cups water
- 2 teaspoons extra-virgin olive oil
- 1 lemon
- ⅛ teaspoon salt
- ⅛ teaspoon freshly ground black pepper

Instructions:
1. Use a sharp knife to trim the ends of the artichoke so that the bases are flat.
2. Place a 3- or 6-quart pressure cooker on top of the stainless steel trivet.
3. Pour 1 ½ cups of water into the bowl to steam.
4. Place the artichokes on the trivet with their flat sides facing up. Knock on the lid.
5. To set the cooking time to 23 minutes at high pressure, use the manual setting. Either the manual release or the natural release can be used.
6. To serve the arthokes, arrange them on a sizable plate using tongs.
7. Squeeze the lemon over the arms and drizzle the olive oil on top. Sprinkle with salt and pepper, then serve right away.

Nutritional Info: Calories 86; Fat 0.3g; Sodium 311mg; Carbs 18.4g; Fiber 9g; Sugar 1.7g; Protein 6.6g

Simple Carrots

Preparation time: 10 minutes
Cooking time: 2 minutes
Serves: 8

Ingredients
- 2 pounds fresh carrots, washed
- 1 cup water
- 1 teaspoon fresh or dried thyme, chopped
- 1 tbsp melted ghee, butter, or coconut oil

Instructions:
1. Cut the carrots into 1-inch cubes.
2. Fill the 6-quart pressure cooker's base with water. Add the rabbits.
3. Close the lid and check that the valve is set to seal.
4. The cook time should be set at 2 minutes on high pressure.
5. When the cooking process is over, carefully quick-release the pressure.
6. Take off the lid and transfer the water and vegetables to a casserole dish.
7. Pour the melted ghee or coconut oil over the drained carrots in a serving dish. Add the thyme and serve warm or at room temperature.

Nutritional Info: Calories 52; Fat 0.7g; Sodium 79mg; Carbs 11.2g; Fiber 3.3g; Sugar 5.5g; Protein 1.3g

Savory Almond Paste

Preparation time: 10 minutes
Cooking time: 15 minutes
Serves: 3

Ingredients
- 1 cup blanched whole almonds
- ½ cup white sugar plus 1 tbsp
- ¼ cup water
- ⅛ teaspoon almond extract

Instructions:
1. In a food processor, blend the almonds until they resemble meal, scraping the sides and bottom of the bowl as necessary. Don't over-process it; at this point, the mixture should still be crumbly rather than paste-like.
2. Combine 12 cups plus 1 tbsp sugar with water in a small saucepan.up to a boil.
3. Next, boil the mixture for 4 minutes at medium heat. Heat it for a further 6 to 8 minutes, or until it reaches 240°F and becomes a medium-thick syrup. The syrup will thicken as it cools if you overcook it.
4. Next, switch off the heat. Add the almonds and almond essence and combine.
5. Turn the heat back on and cook the almond paste for 30 to 60 seconds, or until it holds together, stirring with a spatula and scraping the bottom and sides to prevent burning.
6. Turn off the heat beneath the pan. right away if it is cool enough to handle, or wrap it in waxed paper and store it in an airtight container for up to a few weeks. Alternatively, you can freeze the wrapped almond paste for up to six months by placing it in a freezer bag.

Nutritional Info: Calories 983; Fat 47.5g; Sodium 3mg; Carbs 133g; Fiber 12g; Sugar 117g; Protein 20g

Fried Jalapeno Cornbread

Preparation time: 10 minutes
Cooking time: 20 minutes
Serves: 2

Ingredients
- 1 tbsp flaxseed meal
- 3 tbsps water
- cooking spray
- 1 cup stone-ground yellow cornmeal
- ⅔ cup all-purpose flour
- ¼ cup nutritional yeast
- 2 tbsps white sugar
- 2 ¼ tsp baking powder
- ½ teaspoon ground black pepper
- 1 teaspoon kosher salt
- ⅓ cup vegetable oil
- 1 cup unsweetened almond milk
- 1 large jalapeno pepper, seeded and minced

Instructions:
1. In a small bowl, combine the flaxseed meal and water; stir to combine.After that, allot 10 minutes.
2. In the meantime, heat an air fryer to 350°F as directed by the manufacturer. Put cooking spray into a 6-inch heat-resistant inner pot.
3. In a medium mixing bowl, combine the nutritional yeast, sugar, cornmeal, flour, baking powder, salt, and pepper. Almond milk, oil, and flaxseed-water mixture must all be thoroughly blended before being added. Add the jalapeo and pour the prepared pot into the air fryer.
4. Cook for 15 minutes in a hot air fryer. With tongs, remove the inner pot, turn the cornbread, and air fry for a further five minutes, or until a toothpick inserted in the center comes out clean. Serve warm.

Nutritional Info: Calories 889; Fat 44g; Sodium 1290mg; Carbs 113g; Fiber 14g; Sugar 19g; Protein 21g

Blueberry Muffins

Preparation time: 10 minutes
Cooking time: 35 minutes
Serves: 4

Ingredients
- cooking spray
- 2 cups fresh blueberries
- 2 cups all-purpose flour
- 1 cup lightly packed brown sugar
- ½ cup unsweetened applesauce
- ½ cup soy milk
- ¼ cup soy margarine
- 1 tbsp baking powder
- 1 teaspoon vanilla extract
- ½ teaspoon salt

Instructions:
1. Preheat the oven to 350°F with care.12 mini muffin cups with paper liners or cooking spray on them.
2. In a mixing bowl, combine the following ingredients: salt, baking powder, vanilla extract, blueberries, flour, sugar, applesauce, soy milk, and soy margarine. Half-full muffin tins should be used.
3.Bake for 35 minutes, or until the tops are crisp, in a preheated oven. Allow it to slowly cool on a rack.

Nutritional Info: Calories 683; Fat 13g; Sodium 455mg; Carbs 137g; Fiber 4g; Sugar 84g; Protein 8g

Orange Cake

Preparation time: 10 minutes
Cooking time: 30 minutes
Serves: 3

Ingredients
- 1 large orange, peeled
- 1 ½ cups all-purpose flour
- 1 cup white sugar
- ½ cup vegetable oil
- 1 ½ tsp baking soda
- ¼ teaspoon salt

Instructions:
1. Preheat the oven to 375 degrees Fahrenheit.Butter an 8x8 baking dish.
2. After blending the orange until it is liquefied, measure 1 cup of orange juice.
3. In a mixing bowl, combine the orange juice, flour, sugar, vegetable oil, baking soda, and salt. Carefully layer the batter into the prepared baking dish.
4.Bake for at least 30 minutes. A toothpick should exit the cake's center with no batter attached.

Nutritional Info: Calories 692; Fat 36.7g; Sodium 817mg; Carbs 87g; Fiber 3g; Sugar 38g; Protein 7g

Herbed Mushroom Stuffing

Preparation time: 10 minutes
Cooking time: 1 hour 20 minutes
Serves: 5

Ingredients
- 1 loaf of vegan, gluten-free, brown rice bread (such as Food for Life®), cubed
- 2 tbsps vegan margarine (such as Earth Balance®)
- 1 ½ cups mixed forest mushrooms, diced
- 1 ¼ cups sweet onion, chopped
- 2 ½ tsp dried sage
- 1 ½ tsp dried rosemary
- ½ teaspoon dried thyme
- sea salt, to taste
- freshly ground black pepper to taste
- 6 tbsps vegan margarine (such as Earth Balance®), melted
- 1 ½ cups low-sodium vegan broth
- 8 ounces fresh cranberries
- 1 cup chopped Granny Smith apple, peeled
- ⅓ cup minced fresh parsley

Instructions:
1. Preheat the oven to 350°F with care.
2. Use aluminum foil to line a baking tray.
3. Evenly distribute the bread pieces on the prepared baking sheet lined with foil. In a preheated oven, toast for 10 minutes, or until fragrant and light brown.
4. Move the baking sheet to a cool spot so it can cool. After that, place the cooled bread cubes in an appropriate mixing dish.
5. Melt 2 tbsps of margarine in a big pot over medium heat while the bread is toasting.
6. Add the onions and mushrooms. 7. Cook the mixture for at least five minutes, or until the onions are just beginning to turn translucent. Add a tiny bit of vegetable broth if it needs more moisture, and season to taste with sage, rosemary, thyme, salt, and black pepper. For an additional 2 minutes, stir with a wooden spoon to combine.
7. In a mixing bowl, combine the toasted bread and the mushroom mixture. Toss to distribute evenly. Add the cranberries, apple, and parsley after combining the mixture with 6 tbsps of melted margarine and vegan broth. Then gently but thoroughly blend. Aluminum foil should be placed over the stuffing in a casserole dish.
8. Bake for 45 minutes in a preheated oven; check at 25 minutes to avoid scorching. the top and stir gently.
9. Bake for about 15 minutes, or until the top is golden. Before serving, let it cool for a while.

Nutritional Info: Calories 373; Fat 20g; Sodium 131mg; Carbs 47g; Fiber 6g; Sugar 26g; Protein 6g

Gingerbread Cookies

Preparation time: 10 minutes plus 2 hours for refrigerating
Cooking time: 15 minutes
Serves: 1

Ingredients
- 1 ½ cups all-purpose flour
- 1 teaspoon baking powder
- 1 teaspoon ground cinnamon
- ½ teaspoon baking soda
- ½ teaspoon ground ginger
- ½ teaspoon ground allspice
- ¼ teaspoon salt
- ½ cup coconut oil, at room temperature
- ⅓ cup molasses
- ¼ cup white sugar
- 1 teaspoon vanilla extract

Instructions:
1. Preheat the oven to 350°F with care. Prepare two baking trays with parchment paper linings.
2. In a mixing basin, combine the baking powder, flour, baking soda, cinnamon, ginger, allspice, and salt.
3. Add the vanilla extract to the mixture of sugar, molasses, and coconut oil. 4. For about 2 minutes, or until a sticky dough develops, add the flour mixture. The dough should spend two hours in the refrigerator after being wrapped in plastic wrap.
4. On a floured surface, roll the dough into a 14 to 12-inch thickness. Lay out the cookies on the oven sheets after using a floured cookie cutter to make them.
5. Bake for 8 to 10 minutes, or until lightly browned.

Nutritional Info: Calories 2050; Fat 111g; Sodium 1264mg; Carbs 252g; Fiber 7g; Sugar 104g; Protein 19.6g

Vegan Cashew Macaroni and Cheese

Preparation time: 10 minutes
Cooking time: 45 minutes
Serves: 3

Ingredients
- 1 (8 ounces) package uncooked elbow macaroni
- 1 tbsp vegetable oil
- 1 medium onion, chopped
- 1 cup cashews
- ⅓ cup lemon juice
- 1 ⅓ cups water
- salt to taste
- ⅓ cup canola oil
- 4 ounces roasted red peppers, drained
- 3 tbsps nutritional yeast
- 1 teaspoon garlic powder
- 1 teaspoon onion powder

Instructions:
1. Preheat the oven to 350°F with care.
2. Heat up a large pot of water that has been lightly seasoned.
3. Stir in the macaroni. 4. Cook until al dente, which takes at least 8 to 10 minutes. Then flush. Put it inside a medium baking pan.
4. Place a medium pot on the stove and heat to medium-low. The vegetable oil is warmed.
5. Throw in an onion. Cook the onion until it is tender and lightly browned. Fold the macaroni in slowly.
6. Use a blender or food processor to incorporate cashews, lemon juice, water, and salt. Add the nutritional yeast, roasted red peppers, canola oil, garlic powder, and onion powder gradually to the mixture. Blend until the mixture is flawless. Pasta and onions should be well combined.
7. Bake for 45 minutes, or until lightly browned, in a preheated oven. Before serving, let the food cool for 10 to 15 minutes.

Nutritional Info: Calories 814; Fat 53g; Sodium 1277mg; Carbs 66g; Fiber 5.6g; Sugar 11g; Protein 24g

Basil Oatmeal Patties

Preparation time: 10 minutes
Cooking time: 15 minutes
Serves: 5

Ingredients
- 4 cups water
- 4 cups quick-cooking oats
- ½ onion, chopped
- ⅓ cup vegetable oil
- ½ cup spaghetti sauce
- ½ cup chopped pecans
- ¼ cup nutritional yeast
- 2 tsp garlic powder
- 1 teaspoon dried basil
- 2 tsp onion powder
- 1 teaspoon ground coriander
- 1 teaspoon sage
- 1 teaspoon active dry yeast

Instructions:
1. Preheat the oven to 350°F with care. Greasing a baking sheet is necessary.
2. Add the oatmeal to a pot of boiling water.
3. Reduce the heat to low and cover. Cook for 5 to 10 minutes, or until the oats are soft and the water has been absorbed.
4. After that, turn off the heat and let the oatmeal sit for 5 minutes.
5. Combine the oats with the onion, oil, spaghetti sauce, pecans, nutritional yeast, basil, coriander, onion powder, garlic powder, and active yeast. After completely combining, shape the patties.
6. Arrange the patties evenly on the baking sheet that has been buttered.
7. After 30 minutes of baking, turn the dish over once to the other side.
8. Serve and enjoy!

Nutritional Info: Calories 317; Fat 23.6g; Sodium 442mg; Carbs 30g; Fiber 8g; Sugar 3g; Protein 11g

Salads and Sides Recipes

Lemony Greek Salad

Preparation time: 10 minutes
Cooking time: None
Serves: 4

Ingredients
- 1 head iceberg lettuce
- 1 head romaine lettuce
- 1 pound plump tomatoes
- 6 ounces Greek or black olives, sliced
- 4 ounces sliced radishes
- 4 ounces low-fat feta or goat cheese
- 2 ounces anchovies (optional)

Dressing:
- 3 ounces olive oil or avocado oil
- 3 ounces fresh lemon juice
- 1 teaspoon dried oregano
- 1 teaspoon black pepper
- 1 teaspoon salt
- 4 cloves garlic, minced

Instructions:
1. Lettuce needs to be cleaned before being sliced into little pieces. Quartering tomatoes is recommended.
2. Combine the olives, lettuce, tomatoes, and radishes in a sizable mixing basin. 3. The dressing's components should be combined with the veggies.
3. Half-fill a small serving bowl with the ingredients. Top the crumbles of feta or goat cheese with anchovy fillets (if desired).

Nutritional Info: Calories 407; Fat 32g; Sodium 1607mg; Carbs 23g; Fiber 8.8g; Sugar 8g; Protein 12g

Cucumber and Quinoa Tabbouleh

Preparation time: 10 minutes
Cooking time: None
Serves: 2

Ingredients
- 1 cup cooked quinoa mixed
- 1 tbsp sesame seeds
- ½ cup chopped tomato and green pepper
- 1 cup chopped cucumber
- ½ cup chopped cilantro

Dressing:
- 1 tbsp olive oil or cumin oil
- 1 tbsp fresh lemon juice
- 1 pinch black pepper
- 1 pinch sea salt

Instructions:
1. In a large mixing bowl, combine all of the ingredients.

Nutritional Info: Calories 237; Fat 11.6g; Sodium 741mg; Carbs 29g; Fiber 5g; Sugar 6.6g; Protein 6g

Mayo Pasta Salad

Preparation time: 15 minutes plus 2 hours for refrigerating
Cooking time: 15 minutes
Serves: 5

Ingredients
- 1 (16 ounces) package dried rotini pasta
- 1 ½ cups medium chunky salsa
- 1 cup mayonnaise
- ½ cup sour cream
- 1 (16 ounces) can black beans, rinsed and drained
- 1 (11 ounces) can Mexican-style corn with red and green peppers, drained
- ½ cup chopped red bell pepper
- 2 green onions, sliced thin
- 1 (4.25-ounce) can slice black olives, drained
- ½ teaspoon garlic powder
- ½ teaspoon ground cumin, or to taste
- ½ teaspoon dried cilantro, or to taste
- 1 teaspoon salt
- ground black pepper to taste

Instructions:
1. Boil some mildly salted water in a large pot, add the rotini, and cook for 8 minutes, or until the pasta is tender to the bite but still hard to the bite. Drain. Rinse thoroughly until completely cool under cold running water.
2. Toss the cold pasta with the mixture of the salsa, mayonnaise, sour cream, black beans, Mexican-style corn, red bell pepper, green onions, black olives, cumin, cilantro, salt, and pepper in a large mixing dish. 3. Before serving, place the bowl in the refrigerator, wrapped in plastic.

Nutritional Info: Calories 920; Fat 23.6g; Sodium 1907mg; Carbs 151g; Fiber 30g; Sugar 8g; Protein 32g

Broccoli-Crab Salad with Rotini

Preparation time: 4 minutes
Cooking time: 20 minutes
Serves: 3

Ingredients
- 1 pound uncooked tri-color rotini pasta
- 1 tbsp extra-virgin olive oil
- 1 green bell pepper, seeded and diced
- 2 cups broccoli florets
- 1 cup diced carrots
- 8 ounces fresh crabmeat, well picked over
- 2 ounces sliced black olives, drained
- 3 tbsps minced sweet onion
- 1 cup mayonnaise
- 6 tbsps balsamic vinaigrette salad dressing
- 1 teaspoon of dried Italian herb seasoning
- ⅛ teaspoon ground black pepper, or to taste
- ¼ cup cherry tomatoes for garnish

Instructions:
1. Cook the rotini for 8 minutes, or until cooked through but still firm to the bite, in a good saucepan with lightly salted water that has been heated to boiling. In a sizable mixing bowl, combine the drained pasta with extra virgin olive oil. While you prepare the other ingredients, place the food in the refrigerator for about 30 minutes.
2. Combine the bell pepper, broccoli, carrots, crabmeat, olives, and onion in a mixing bowl.Combine spaghetti with
3. In a separate bowl, combine the dressing ingredients—mayonnaise, balsamic vinaigrette, Italian seasoning, and black pepper—and whisk. Pour the dressing over the pasta salad. Blend everything together.
4. Top with cherry tomatoes and serve chilled or at room temperature.

Nutritional Info: Calories 712; Fat 45.5g; Sodium 1475mg; Carbs 53.5g; Fiber 11g; Sugar 5g; Protein 24.6g

Salmon-Shallot Pasta Salad

Preparation time: 4 minutes
Cooking time: 20 minutes
Serves: 2

Ingredients
- ½ (16 ounces) package mezze (short) penne pasta
- 1 cup sliced and quartered cucumber
- 1 cup halved cherry tomatoes
- 2 tbsps minced shallot
- 1 (2.6 ounces) pouch of wild-caught pink salmon (such as Chicken of the Sea®)

Vinaigrette:
- ¼ cup extra-virgin olive oil
- 1 tbsp white wine vinegar
- 1 tbsp of freshly squeezed lemon juice
- 1 teaspoon lemon-pepper seasoning
- ½ teaspoon Dijon mustard
- ½ teaspoon salt
- ¼ teaspoon dried dill weed

Instructions:
1. Warm a large pot of lightly salted water. For about 10 minutes, boil the penne, stirring periodically, until it is tender but not mushy. Served in a serving dish after draining and rinsing with cool water.
2. Toss the spaghetti with the cucumbers, tomatoes, and shallots. Broken-up salmon should be scattered on top.
3. To make the vinaigrette, whisk together the olive oil, vinegar, lemon juice, lemon-pepper seasoning, mustard, salt, and dill in a small mixing dish. Sprinkle the dressing over the salad and gently toss to combine.

Nutritional Info: Calories 470; Fat 31g; Sodium 763mg; Carbs 38g; Fiber 7g; Sugar 3.8g; Protein 12g

Lemony Almond-Arugula Salad

Preparation time: 4 minutes
Cooking time: None
Serves: 2

Ingredients
- 1 cup cooked quinoa
- 1 tbsp pumpkin seeds
- ½ cup chopped almonds
- 1 cup chopped arugula
- ½ cup sliced red peppers

Dressing:
- 1 tbsp olive oil or cumin oil
- 1 tbsp fresh lemon juice
- 1 pinch black pepper
- 1 pinch sea salt

Instructions:
1. In a sizable mixing bowl, combine all the ingredients.

Nutritional Info: Calories 626; Fat 37g; Sodium 1711mg; Carbs 57.8g; Fiber 14g; Sugar 6.5g; Protein 22g

Tortellini and Veggies Salad

Preparation time: 4 minutes
Cooking time: 20 minutes
Serves: 2

Ingredients
- 1 (9 ounces) package cheese tortellini
- 1 small red bell pepper, julienned
- ¾ cup broccoli florets, blanched
- ⅓ cup shredded carrots
- ⅓ cup pitted green olives
- 1 clove garlic, chopped
- ½ cup mayonnaise
- ¼ cup prepared basil pesto
- ¼ cup milk
- 2 tbsps grated Parmesan cheese
- 1 tbsp olive oil
- 1 tbsp distilled white vinegar
- 1 bunch fresh spinach leaves

Instructions:
1. Warm a large pot of lightly salted water. Tortellini should be cooked for 7 to 8 minutes, or until tender. After draining, cool.
2. Combine the cooked tortellini, red bell pepper, broccoli, carrots, olives, and garlic in a large mixing bowl.
3. Combine the mayonnaise, pesto, milk, Parmesan cheese, vinegar, and olive oil separately. The pasta and vegetables should be coated with sauce. Refrigerate for an hour, covered, or until cool. On top of the spinach leaves, plate.

Nutritional Info: Calories 751; Fat 38g; Sodium 1246mg; Carbs 75g; Fiber 8.6g; Sugar 6.5g; Protein 29g

Lemony Shrimp Salad with Pasta Shell

Preparation time: 10 minutes plus 2 to 3 hours
Cooking time: 15 minutes
Serves: 4

Ingredients
- 1 ¼ cups mayonnaise, or more if needed
- 2 tsp Dijon mustard
- 2 tsp ketchup
- ¼ teaspoon Worcestershire sauce
- 1 teaspoon salt, or to taste
- 1 pinch of cayenne pepper, or to taste
- 1 lemon, juiced
- ⅓ cup chopped fresh dill

Salad:
- 1 (12 ounces) package small pasta shells
- 1 pound cooked, peeled, and deveined small shrimp, cut in half
- ½ cup finely diced red bell pepper
- ¾ cup diced celery
- salt and ground black pepper to taste
- 1 pinch of paprika for garnish
- 3 sprigs fresh dill, or as desired

Instructions:
1. In a mixing dish, combine 1: Combine 1: 14 cups mayonnaise, 13 cups chopped dill, 14 cups Dijon mustard, 14 cups ketchup, 14 cups Worcestershire sauce, salt, and cayenne pepper. Stir until thoroughly combined. Refrigerate.
2. Boil salted water in a pot, add the pasta shells, and simmer for 8 to 10 minutes, or until tender. Pasta should be drained, then rinsed in cold water to give it a slight chill. Place it in a big mixing basin.
3. Toss the spaghetti and shrimp together with the red bell pepper, celery, and dressing. Pour dressing into shells once fully combined. Put the bowl in the fridge for two to three hours with plastic wrap on top.
4. Add extra salt, black pepper, lemon juice, and cayenne pepper to taste before serving. 5. Add a little extra mayonnaise if the salad seems to be on the dry side. Add paprika and dill sprigs as a garnish.

Nutritional Info: Calories 453; Fat 26g; Sodium 1875mg; Carbs 32g; Fiber 6g; Sugar 3g; Protein 23g

Pomegranate Walnut Salad

Preparation time: 10 minutes
Cooking time: None
Serves: 1

Ingredients
- 3 cups leafy salad green mix
- ½ cup pomegranate seeds
- ⅓ cup crumbled blue cheese
- ¼ cup crushed walnuts
- ¼ cup cranberry vinaigrette

Instructions:
1. In a medium salad bowl, combine the leafy greens, blue cheese, walnuts, and pomegranate seeds. cranberry vinaigrette right before serving.

Nutritional Info: Calories 468; Fat 28g; Sodium 565mg; Carbs 44g; Fiber 10g; Sugar 29g; Protein 17.5g

Sesame Tomato, Cucumber, and Quinoa Salad

Preparation time: 10 minutes
Cooking time: None
Serves: 2

Ingredients
- 1 cup cooked quinoa
- 1 tbsp sesame seeds
- 1 cup cooked chickpeas
- 1 cup chopped cucumber and green onions
- ½ cup chopped tomato

Dressing:
- 1 tbsp olive oil or avocado oil
- 1 tbsp fresh lemon juice
- 1 pinch black pepper
- 1 pinch sea salt

Instructions:
1. In a sizable mixing bowl, combine all the ingredients.

Nutritional Info: Calories 321; Fat 9.7g; Sodium 857mg; Carbs 48g; Fiber 11g; Sugar 7g; Protein 13g

Sesame Almonds, Strawberry, and Spinach Salad

Preparation time: 8 minutes
Cooking time: None
Serves: 4 to 6

Ingredients
- 2 tbsps black sesame seeds
- 1 tbsp poppy seeds
- ½ cup olive oil or avocado oil
- ¼ cup lemon juice
- ¼ teaspoon paprika
- 1 bag fresh spinach, chopped, washed, and dried
- 1-quart strawberries, sliced
- ¼ cup toasted slivered almonds

Instructions:
1. Lettuce needs to be cleaned before being sliced into little pieces. Quartering tomatoes is recommended.
2. Combine the olives, lettuce, tomatoes, and radishes in a sizable mixing basin. 3. The dressing's components should be combined with the veggies.
3. Half-fill a small serving bowl with the ingredients.
4. Top the crumbled feta or goat cheese with anchovy fillets (if desired).

Nutritional Info: Calories 274; Fat 25g; Sodium 49mg; Carbs 12.7g; Fiber 4.4g; Sugar 6g; Protein 3g

Cauliflower & Eggs Salad

Preparation time: 8 minutes
Cooking time: None
Serves: 3

Ingredients
- 1 cup chopped cauliflower
- 2 hardboiled eggs, chopped,
- 2 ounces shredded cheddar cheese, low-fat
- 1 red onion
- 1 dill pickles
- 1 tbsp yellow mustard.

Instructions:
1. In a sizable salad bowl, combine all the ingredients.

Nutritional Info: Calories 351; Fat 17g; Sodium 2050mg; Carbs 27g; Fiber 6g; Sugar 13g; Protein 24.7g

Asparagus-Quinoa Salad

Preparation time: 10 minutes
Cooking time: None
Serves: 2

Ingredients
- 1 cup cooked quinoa
- 1 tbsp sunflower seeds
- 1 cup sliced red peppers
- 1 cup grilled asparagus
- lime and parsley, to garnish

Dressing:
- 1 tbsp olive oil or avocado oil
- 1 tbsp fresh lemon juice
- 1 pinch black pepper
- 1 pinch sea salt

Instructions:
1. In a sizable mixing bowl, combine all the ingredients.

Nutritional Info: Calories 240; Fat 11g; Sodium 604mg; Carbs 30g; Fiber 6g; Sugar 4.6g; Protein 7.8g

Avocado-Cobb Salad

Preparation time: 4 minutes
Cooking time: 20 minutes
Serves: 5

Ingredients
- 6 tbsps oil, plus more for grilling
- 3 tbsps red wine vinegar
- 1 tbsp Dijon mustard
- 1 teaspoon honey
- 1 clove garlic, minced
- Salt and pepper
- 1 large head green leaf lettuce halved (5 Cup yield)
- 2 ripe vine tomatoes halved
- 2 firm avocados
- 2 ears corn, whole and cleaned
- 1 package Grimm's Bacon and Cheddar Bavarian Smokies
- 4 hardboiled eggs, diced
- ½ cup Grimm's Medium Cheddar Cheese, grated
- Grimm's Cheese tortilla wraps, grilled.

Instructions:
1. Get your grill ready. In a small bowl, combine 6 tbsps of oil, red wine vinegar, Dijon, honey, and garlic. Set aside after seasoning with salt and pepper.
2. Add salt, pepper, and 2 tbsps of oil to the lettuce halves. 3. Toss the tomato halves in two tbsps of oil and season with salt and pepper. Keep the avocado seeds in their shells after removing the seeds. Oil, salt, and pepper are used to season the interior of the avocados. 2 tbsps of oil, salt, and pepper should be added to the corn.
3. Grill the corn and smokies on the grill, roasting and charring the outsides. Next, sear the lettuce, tomatoes, and avocados' insides over high heat, leaving the outsides largely uncooked. You only care about the scorched taste.
4. Take everything off the grill. 5. The tomatoes should be diced, the corn should be cut from the cob, and the avocados should be sliced. Smokies should be cut into half-moons. It's time to assemble everything at this point.
5. Arrange the charred lettuce first, then a row of tomatoes, hardboiled eggs, sliced smokeies, cheddar, avocados, and corn on a large platter. Serve with grilled tortillas and red wine vinaigrette.

Nutritional Info: Calories 987; Fat 80g; Sodium 901mg; Carbs 41.5g; Fiber 12g; Sugar 9g; Protein 30g

Basil Fiesta Salad

Preparation time: 15 minutes
Cooking time: 30 minutes
Serves: 4

Ingredients
- 2 lemons, juiced, divided
- 1 bunch of fresh basil leaves, divided
- 2 cloves garlic, crushed and peeled
- 2 tbsps olive oil, divided
- 1 tbsp shredded Parmesan cheese, or to taste
- salt and ground black pepper to taste
- ½ pound skinless, boneless chicken thighs
- 1 small onion, thinly sliced
- 2 tbsps vinegar
- 1 tbsp honey
- 1 (8 ounces) package kale, ribs removed and leaves torn into pieces
- 1 English cucumber, cubed
- 1 large heirloom tomato, cubed
- 1 large carrot, cubed
- 1 cup fresh corn kernels
- ½ (15 ounces) can black beans, rinsed and drained
- ½ (6 ounces) can black olives

Instructions:
1. Preheat the oven to 375 degrees Fahrenheit.
2. Blend half a lemon's juice, half the basil, 1 tbsp of olive oil, Parmesan cheese, salt, and pepper in a food processor until smooth. The chicken thighs should be placed in a non-stick baking dish.
3. Roast chicken thighs in a preheated oven for 30 minutes. The chicken should be taken out of the oven and covered with the combined mixture.
4. Bake the chicken once again for 15 minutes, or until the juices run clear and the middle is no longer pink. Allow 10 minutes for cooling. Shred the chicken using two forks. Set aside
5. Heat the remaining olive oil in a skillet over medium-low heat. About 10 minutes of cooking time is required to fully cook and brown the onion. In a mixing dish, combine the remaining basil, lemon juice, vinegar, and honey. The salad must be fully heated in 5 minutes.
6. In a large mixing bowl, combine the chicken, kale, cucumber, tomato, carrot, corn, black beans, and olives.
7. Work heated dressing into the salad and toss to evenly coat.

Nutritional Info: Calories 453; Fat 12.8g; Sodium 323mg; Carbs 59.7g; Fiber 14g; Sugar 12.4g; Protein 30g

Spinach Bean Soup

Preparation time: 10 minutes
Cooking time: 22 minutes
Servings: 6

Ingredients
- Minced garlic: 2 tbsp.
- Cumin: 1 tsp.
- Canned tomatoes, diced: 15 oz., with liquid
- Pepper: ¼ tsp.
- Canned vegetable broth: 14.5 oz., low-sodium
- 1 small onion (chopped)
- Canned chickpeas: 16 oz., with liquid
- Fresh spinach: 4 cups, packed

Instructions:
1. Heat some oil in a medium saucepan over medium heat.
2. Cook for 5 minutes with the onion and garlic.
3. Add the remaining ingredients, except the spinach, and bring to a boil.
4. Reduce the heat, add the spinach, and let it simmer for 10 to 15 minutes before serving.

Nutritional Info: Calories: 95 kcal; Fat 17.2 g; Carbs 17 g; Protein 6 g

Vegetable-Barley Soup

Preparation time: 15 minutes
Cooking time: 15 minutes
Servings: 4

Ingredients
- Half onion, diced
- 1 celery rib
- 1 ½ cups of mixed vegetables, frozen
- 1 cup of chopped kale
- 1 minced garlic clove
- 1 tsp. Of olive oil
- Canned diced tomatoes: 15 oz., with liquid
- Water: half cup
- 1 ½ cups of vegetable broth, low-sodium
- Dried basil: half tsp.
- ⅛ tsp. Of pepper
- Dried oregano: half tsp.
- ¼ cup of barley

Instructions:
1. Heat the oil in a Dutch oven over medium heat and sauté the celery and onion for three minutes.
2. Add the garlic and heat it for 10 seconds. Add the other ingredients, let it come to a boil, then reduce the heat and simmer for 10 to 12 minutes. Serve

Nutritional Info: Calories: 261 kcal; Fat: 13.5 g; Carbs: 11 g; Protein: 4 g

Tomato Basil Soup

Preparation time: 20 minutes
Cooking time: 15 minutes
Servings: 6

Ingredients
- Non-fat milk: 2 cups
- Salt, a pinch
- Garlic powder: half tsp.
- 3 cans of (~14 oz.) Diced tomatoes, salt-free
- Pepper: half tsp.
- Fresh basil: 1 ½ cups

Instructions:
1. In a pan, combine all of the ingredients except the baking soda.
2. Bring to a boil, then reduce to a low heat and cook for 15 minutes.
3. Garnish with birch leaves. For five minutes, cook.
4. Blend with an impression blender, then serve.

Nutritional Info: Calories: 79 kcal; Fat 0 g; Carbs 14 g; Protein 5 g

Turkey & Vegetable Barley Soup

Preparation time: 20 minutes
Cooking time: 20 minutes
Servings: 6

Ingredients
- 5 carrots, chopped
- Baby spinach: 2 cups
- 1 onion, chopped
- Cooked turkey breast: 2 cups, cubed
- Pepper: half tsp.
- Canola oil: 1 tbsp.
- Quick-cooking barley: ⅔ cup
- Chicken broth: 6 cups, low-sodium

Instructions:
1. Saute carrots and onion in hot oil for 4 to 5 minutes.
2. Combine the remaining ingredients in a mixing bowl. Allow it to boil for ten to fifteen minutes, then reduce the heat.

Nutritional Info: Calories: 208 kcal; Fat 4 g; Carbs 23 g; Protein 21 g

Mint Almond-Quinoa Tabbouleh

Preparation time: 10 minutes
Cooking time: 20 minutes
Serves: 2 to 3

Ingredients
- 2 cups cooked quinoa
- 1 bunch mint, leaves picked
- 1 bunch flat-leaf parsley
- ½ small red onion, finely chopped
- ¼ cup lemon juice
- ¼ cup extra-virgin olive oil or avocado oil
- ½ cup whole almonds
- ½ cup chia or sunflower seeds
- 1 cup cherry tomatoes
- 1 avocado, optional
- 1 cup chopped kale or dandelion
- low-fat yogurt, to serve, optional

Instructions:
1. Cook the quinoa and set it aside to cool. Chop off and discard the top half of the parsley stalks. Mint, leaves, and the remaining bunch of parsley should all be coarsely chopped.
2. In a salad bowl, mix the herbs with the onion. Add the mixture to the drained quinoa.
3. Use olive oil and lemon juice to season everything well. Season the salad after combining the remaining ingredients.

Nutritional Info: Calories 619; Fat 43g; Sodium 50mg; Carbs 51g; Fiber 13g; Sugar 10g; Protein 14g

Lemony Tuna Tomato Salad

Preparation time: 8 minutes
Cooking time: None
Serves: 1

Ingredients
- 1 can tuna in water, drained
- ⅓ cup four bean mix (or just white or red beans), drained, rinsed
- 1 tomato, deseeded, chopped
- 1 large celery stick, trimmed, finely chopped
- ½ small onion, halved, thinly sliced
- ½ cup flat-leaf parsley leaves, chopped
- ½ lemon, rind finely grated, juiced
- 1 garlic clove, crushed
- 1 tbsp extra-virgin olive oil

Instructions:
1. Combine all ingredients in a mixing bowl, then plate.

Nutritional Info: Calories 399; Fat 17g; Sodium 661mg; Carbs 26g; Fiber 7.5g; Sugar 5.7g; Protein 39g

Spinach Loaded Salad

Preparation time: 4 minutes
Cooking time: 20 minutes
Serves: 1

Ingredients
- 1 cup spinach
- 1 cup shredded cabbage
- yogurt dressing
- cayenne pepper (optional)
- few sprigs of cilantro (optional)
- 2 spring (green) onions
- 5 ounces low-fat farmers cheese

Instructions:
1. Add the yogurt dressing to a serving bowl for the salad.
2. Include the farmers' cheese completely. Spring onions should be chopped into small pieces and added to the cheese mixture. Add the spinach and cabbage, stirring well.
3. Use seasonings (optional).

Nutritional Info: Calories 514; Fat 31g; Sodium 1168mg; Carbs 15.6g; Fiber 4g; Sugar 7.7g; Protein 44.8g

Avocado Side Salad

Preparation time: 10 minutes
Cooking time: 0 minutes
Servings: 4

Ingredients:
- 4 blood oranges, slice into segments
- 2 tbsp. olive oil
- Pinch red pepper, crushed
- 2 avocados, peeled, cut into wedges
- 1 and ½ cups baby arugula
- ¼ cup almonds, toasted and chopped
- 1 tbsp. lemon juice

Instructions:
1. In a salad bowl, combine all of the ingredients and thoroughly shake.

Nutritional Info: Calories: 61 kcal; Fat: 3.7 g; Carbs: 0.2 g; Protein: 6.6 g

Grilled Asparagus-Spinach Salad

Preparation time: 8 minutes
Cooking time: 10 minutes
Serves: 1

Ingredients
- ¼ cup olive oil
- ⅛ cup lemon juice
- 12 fresh asparagus spears
- 6 cups fresh spinach leaves
- ⅛ cup grated Parmesan cheese
- 1 tbsp seasoned slivered almonds

Instructions:
1. Start a grill at a medium-low temperature.
2. Lemon juice and olive oil should be combined in a dish. In the dish, twirl the asparagus to coat.
3. After 5 minutes, flip the asparagus and brush it with the olive oil mixture. Return to the oil-covered plate after removing it from the grill.
4. In a sizable mixing bowl, combine the spinach, Parmesan cheese, and slivered almonds. After cutting the asparagus into bite-sized pieces, toss it with the salad's oil and lemon juice. After combining, serve.

Nutritional Info: Calories 596; Fat 59g; Sodium 379mg; Carbs 12.4g; Fiber 5g; Sugar 2.4g; Protein 10g

Beans and Corn Salad

Preparation time: 4 minutes
Cooking time: None
Serves: 6

Ingredients
- 1 (1 ounce) package of dry ranch dressing mix (such as Hidden Valley Ranch®)
- 1 cup buttermilk
- 1 cup fat-free plain yogurt
- ½ (1.25 ounce) package of taco seasoning mix, or more to taste

Salad:
- 8 cups torn romaine lettuce
- 2 roasted red peppers, diced
- 1 (14 ounces) can black beans, rinsed and drained
- 1 (14 ounces) can white corn, drained
- ¼ cup finely chopped sweet onion
- 1 (4 ounces) can dice green chile peppers
- 1 cup diced Roma tomatoes
- ½ cup shredded sharp Cheddar cheese
- 1 large avocado, peeled, pitted, and sliced
- ¼ cup chopped fresh cilantro (optional)

Instructions:
1. In a bowl, combine the taco seasoning mix, buttermilk, yogurt, and dressing mix.
2. Place the lettuce in a sizable serving bowl.
3. In a mixing dish, combine roasted peppers, black beans, corn, onions, and green chiles. On top of the lettuce, spread the mixture. Add tomatoes on top, then top with Cheddar cheese. Slices of avocado should be placed in a circle and should overlap. If desired, add cilantro as a garnish. Serving the dressing separately is appropriate.

Nutritional Info: Calories 465; Fat 12g; Sodium 598mg; Carbs 69.5g; Fiber 17g; Sugar 12.8g; Protein 25g

Chicken and Greens Salads

Preparation time: 4 minutes
Cooking time: 20 minutes
Serves: 5

Ingredients
- 10 ounces cucumber ranch salad dressing
- 2 tbsps Buffalo-style hot pepper sauce (such as Frank's® RedHot)
- 4 stalks of celery, cut into ⅛-inch slices
- 4 medium carrots, cut into ⅛-inch slices
- 15 ounces cooked chicken, cut into bite-sized pieces
- 10 cups salad greens
- 1 ¼ cups crumbled blue cheese
- ¾ cup croutons (optional)

Instructions:
1. Combine ranch dressing and spicy sauce in a small bowl.
2. Divide the dressing into five quart-sized glass canning jars with wide mouths to create the first layer. Equal parts of carrots and celery should be used to create the next two layers.
3. Add 3 ounces of chicken to each container. Then 2 cups of salad greens are placed on top of the chicken in each jar, and ¼ cup of blue cheese is added. Store the jars in the refrigerator until needed.
4. Equivalently distribute the croutons among the five little lidded jars. When you're ready to eat, combine the jar's contents with the croutons in a bowl.

Nutritional Info: Calories 616; Fat 47g; Sodium 1222mg; Carbs 15.3g; Fiber 4.2g; Sugar 5.8g; Protein 33.3g

Tasty Celery Root Salad

Preparation time: 2 hours
Cooking time: 20 minutes
Serves: 1

Ingredients
- 1 pound celery root
- 3 tbsps rapeseed oil
- 2 tbsps lemon juice
- 1 tbsp white wine vinegar
- salt to taste
- freshly ground black pepper to taste

Instructions:
1. After peeling the celery root, cut it into quarters.Place in a pot of lightly salted water.
2.After bringing the water to a boil, reduce the heat to low and simmer the potatoes for around 20 minutes. Set aside to cool completely after draining.Slice into pieces and place in a salad bowl.
3. In a small dish, mix the oil, lemon juice, vinegar, salt, and pepper. Celery root should be covered with the dressing. To allow flavors to meld, let the food marinate for at least two hours.

Nutritional Info: Calories 443; Fat 41.6g; Sodium 364mg; Carbs 15.6g; Fiber 7g; Sugar 6.8g; Protein 3g

Dijon Red Leaf Salad

Preparation time: 10 minutes
Cooking time: None
Serves: 1

Ingredients
- 1 head red leaf lettuce
- 1 red bell pepper, chopped
- 1 stalk green onion, thinly sliced

Dressing:
- 3 tbsps extra-virgin olive oil
- 1 tbsp red wine vinegar
- 1 tbsp balsamic vinegar
- 1 tbsp lemon juice
- ½ teaspoon salt, or to taste
- ¼ teaspoon Dijon mustard, or more to taste
- freshly ground black pepper to taste

Instructions:
1. Clean and separate the red leaf lettuce leaves with a salad spinner.Cut the leaves into bite-sized pieces, then put them in a salad bowl with the bell pepper and scallions.
2. In a resealable container, combine the following ingredients: olive oil, red wine vinegar, balsamic vinegar, lemon juice, salt, mustard, and pepper. Close the lid and shake to combine.
3. Dress the salad to your liking, then toss to combine. Any dressing that is left should be refrigerated.

Nutritional Info: Calories 455; Fat 41.6g; Sodium 1266mg; Carbs 16.8g; Fiber 4.3g; Sugar 7g; Protein 5.5g

Kale, White Been & Tomato Sorghum Soup

Preparation time: 15 minutes
Cooking time: 25 minutes
Servings: 10

Ingredients
- Chicken broth: 7 cups, low-sodium
- Kosher salt & pepper: ¼ tsp. Each
- Olive oil: 1 tbsp.
- Whole grain sorghum: half cup, uncooked
- 2 chopped garlic cloves
- Hot sauce: 1 tsp.
- 1 onion, chopped
- 1 can of (15 oz.) Diced tomatoes, undrained
- Kale: 12 oz., chopped without stems
- 2 cans of (15 oz.) white beans, rinsed

Instructions:
1. Bring three cups of broth to a boil in a saucepan.
2. Sorghum should be added and simmered for 20 to 25 minutes. It is okay if there is liquid present.
3. Add oil to the mixture in a skillet.4. Garlic, pepper, salt, and onion should be sautéed for 6 to 8 minutes.
4. Add the curry powder and the kale, and simmer for 4 minutes.
5. Place half a cup of beans in a food processor and mash until smooth.
6. Add the other ingredients, including the mashed beans, to the soup.
7. Stir well. Let it come to a boil, then reduce the heat and simmer for 20 minutes. Serve

Nutritional Info: Calories: 175 kcal; Fat: 2 g; Carbs: 30 g; Protein: 10 g

Cauliflower Lunch Salad

Preparation time: 2 hours
Cooking time: 10 minutes
Servings: 4

Ingredients:
- ⅓ cup low-sodium veggie stock
- 2 tbsp. olive oil
- 6 cups cauliflower florets, grated
- Black pepper, to the taste
- ¼ cup red onion, chopped
- 1 red bell pepper, chopped
- Juice ½ lemon
- ½ cup Kalamata olives, halved
- 1 tsp. mint, chopped
- 1 tbsp. cilantro, chopped

Instructions:
1. Use a medium-high heat and a medium-skillet to heat the oil. When adding the cauliflower, pepper, and stock, stir occasionally while cooking for 10 minutes.
2. Transfer to a bowl and freeze for at least two hours before serving.
3. Combine the cooked cauliflower with the olive oil, onion, bell pepper, black pepper, black pepper, cilantro, lemon juice, and black pepper.
4. Serv.

Nutritional Info: Calories: 102 kcal; Fat: 10 g; Carbs: 3 g; Protein: 0 g

Squid And Shrimp Salad

Preparation time: 11 minutes
Cooking time: 15 minutes
Servings: 4

Ingredients:
- 8 oz. squid, cut into medium pieces
- 8 oz. shrimp, peeled and deveined
- 1 red onion, sliced
- 1 cucumber, chopped
- 2 tomatoes, cut into medium wedges
- 2 tbsp. cilantro, chopped
- 1 hot jalapeno pepper, cut in rounds
- 3 tbsp. rice vinegar
- 3 tbsp. dark sesame oil
- Black pepper to the taste

Instructions:
1. In a mixing bowl, combine the onion, cucumber, tomatoes, pepper, cilantro, shrimp, and squid and toss well. Slice a large piece of church paper in half, fold it into a heart shape, and then unfold it. Place the seafood mixture on the baking sheet, fold it over, seal the edges, and bake at 400°F for 15 minutes.
2. In the meantime, combine the same oil, red wine vinegar, and black pepper in a small dish.
3. Take the salad out of the oven and let it cool for a few minutes before serving.
4. Place the cover over the salad and serve immediately.

Nutritional Info: Calories: 235 kcal; Fat: 8.1 g; Carbs: 9 g; Protein: 30 g

Curried Seven-Layer Salad

Preparation time: 1 hour
Cooking time: 15 minutes
Serves: 4

Ingredients
- 2 cups small seashell pasta
- 4 carrots, peeled and julienned
- ½ head leaf lettuce, rinsed, dried, and chopped
- 1 medium cucumber, peeled, seeded, and diced
- ¾ cup frozen green peas
- ½ cup frozen whole-kernel corn
- 2 cups mayonnaise
- 2 tbsps brown sugar
- 1 tbsp curry powder
- ½ teaspoon garlic salt
- 1 cup shredded Cheddar cheese

Instructions:
1. Heat some lightly salted water in a pot. 2. Cook for 7 minutes or until the pasta is tender. To cool, drain and rinse with cold water.
2. Arrange carrots in a single layer in the bottom of a large glass bowl, preferably one with a nearly constant diameter all the way around. The lettuce should be placed on top of the carrots. Over the lettuce, arrange the cucumber, peas, and corn in a layer. Distribute the spaghetti over the top when it has cooled and been drained.
3. In a different small bowl, mix the mayonnaise, brown sugar, curry powder, and garlic salt. Shredded cheddar cheese should then be evenly sprinkled over the spaghetti. Put it in the refrigerator for at least one hour before serving.

Nutritional Info: Calories 698; Fat 50.6g; Sodium 1276mg; Carbs 42g; Fiber 9.6g; Sugar 8.8g; Protein 20.5g

Beef Salad Topping

Preparation time: 8 minutes
Cooking time: 20 minutes
Serves: 2

Ingredients
- ½ cup olive oil
- 1 tbsp soy sauce
- 1 onion, sliced
- 1 green bell pepper, seeded and thinly sliced
- 1 pound beef stew meat, cut into ½ inch pieces

Instructions:
1. In a large saucepan over medium heat, heat the olive oil. In a mixing bowl, combine the soy sauce, onion, and green bell pepper. Cook the vegetables for 3 to 5 minutes, or until they are tender.
2. Stir in the beef stew meat. Cook for 15 minutes, stirring frequently, or until evenly browned.

Nutritional Info: Calories 813; Fat 64.6g; Sodium 309mg; Carbs 9.7g; Fiber 1.4g; Sugar 5g; Protein 51g

Rice and Peas Salad

Preparation time: 10 minutes
Cooking time: 15 minutes
Serves: 6

Ingredients
- 2 cups water
- 1 cup white rice
- 6 eggs
- 1 (10 ounces) package of frozen peas, thawed
- 1 cup chopped celery
- ¼ cup chopped onion
- 1 (4 ounces) jar diced pimento
- 1 cup mayonnaise
- 1 teaspoon prepared mustard
- 1 tbsp lemon juice
- ¼ cup sweet pickle relish
- 1 (9 ounces) can of solid white tuna packed in water, drained
- ¼ teaspoon dried dill weed
- 1 teaspoon salt
- ⅛ teaspoon pepper

Instructions:
1. Bring the water to a boil in a saucepan. rice by stirring. Cook for 20 minutes with the heat reduced to low and the cover on. removing the heat and letting it cool.
2. Fill a pot with eggs halfway with cold water. After bringing it to a boil, turn off the heat. Let the covered eggs sit in the boiling water for 10 to 12 minutes. Before peeling and cutting, remove them from the boiling water and let them cool.
3. Frozen peas should be rinsed in cold water. After straining, put everything in a sizable mixing bowl. Add the celery, onions, pimiento, rice, eggs, and so on. Combine the tuna, dill, mayonnaise, mustard, lemon juice, relish, salt, and pepper in a different mixing dish. Toss the vegetable mixture into the combine. Covered and refrigerated for at least 4 hours. Toss again before serving. Before serving, chill.

Nutritional Info: Calories 412; Fat 19g; Sodium 1054mg; Carbs 36.7g; Fiber 3.7g; Sugar 4.6g; Protein 22g

Ranch-Barbecue Chicken Salad

Preparation time: 15 minutes
Cooking time: 10 minutes
Serves: 6

Ingredients
- 2 skinless, boneless chicken breast halves
- 1 head red leaf lettuce, rinsed and torn
- 1 head green leaf lettuce, rinsed and torn
- 1 fresh tomato, chopped
- 1 bunch cilantro, chopped
- 1 (15.25-ounce) can whole kernel corn, drained
- 1 (15 ounces) can black beans, drained
- 1 (2.8-ounce) can French fried onions
- ½ cup Ranch dressing
- ½ cup barbeque sauce

Instructions:
1. Preheat the grill to high.
2. Lightly coat the grill grate with oil. The chicken should be grilled for six minutes on each side, or until the juices flow clear. slice after removing it from the flame and letting it cool.
3. In a sizable mixing bowl, combine the corn, black beans, tomato, cilantro, red and green leaf lettuce, and tomato. Serve with French fried onions and grilled chicken slices.
In a small bowl, mix the ranch dressing and barbecue sauce. Mix the sauce with the salad to coat it, or serve as a dipping sauce on the side.

Nutritional Info: Calories 503; Fat 12g; Sodium 676mg; Carbs 73g; Fiber 15.6g; Sugar 12.6g; Protein 29g

Mayo Chicken Salad

Preparation time: 10 minutes
Cooking time: 15 minutes
Serves: 5

Ingredients
- cooking spray
- 2 pounds skinless, boneless chicken breast halves
- 1 teaspoon kosher salt, divided
- ¾ teaspoon ground black pepper, divided
- ¾ teaspoon onion powder
- 1 cup mayonnaise, or more to taste
- ½ cup sour cream
- ¼ cup sweet relish
- 3 stalks of green onions (white and light green parts only), minced
- 2 tbsps chopped fresh parsley
- 1 tbsp Dijon mustard
- 1 tbsp lemon juice
- 1 teaspoon dried dill weed
- ½ cup finely chopped celery

Instructions:
1. Preheat the oven to 300 degrees Fahrenheit.Spray some cooking spray in a baking dish.
2. Season the chicken with 12 tsp each of salt, pepper, and onion powder.in the baking dish that has been prepared and tightly cover it with foil.
3. Bake for about 1 hour and 20 minutes; do not overcook the chicken. The juices should run clear. An instant-read thermometer should register at least 165°F in the center.
4. Take the dish out of the oven, cover it, and leave it be for 15 minutes, or until it is cold enough to handle. Any remaining chicken broth should be kept.
5. Prepare the dressing while the chicken cools off. Add 1 cup mayonnaise, 1 cup sour cream, relish, green onions, parsley, Dijon, lemon juice, dill, and the remaining salt and pepper to a large mixing bowl.
6. Put the chicken in the food processor's bowl in large bits. Pulse the chicken 3 to 5 times to achieve the desired level of shreddedness.
7. Put the chicken in a serving dish. Toss the celery with the dressing to coat. Add more mayonnaise or any unused broth if you wish to add more moisture.
8. Chill for at least two hours (or up to two days) before serving. Mix all the ingredients together carefully before serving.

Nutritional Info: Calories 429; Fat 22.7g; Sodium 1082mg; Carbs 9g; Fiber 1.3g; Sugar 4.6g; Protein 45g

Shrimp Salad with Cilantro Vinaigrette

Preparation time: 15 minutes
Cooking time: 20 minutes
Serves: 3

Ingredients
- 1 tbsp olive oil
- 2 ¼ tsp smokehouse maple seasoning (such as McCormick® Grill Mates®)
- 1 ½ tsp lemon juice
- 12 ounces peeled and deveined shrimp

Cilantro Vinaigrette:
- ¼ cup extra-virgin olive oil
- 2 tbsps honey
- 2 tbsps fresh lime juice
- 2 tbsps chopped cilantro
- 1 tbsp balsamic vinegar
- salt and ground black pepper to taste

Salad:
- 4 cups mixed salad greens, or more to taste
- ½ cup thinly sliced English cucumber
- ⅓ cup freshly cooked corn
- ½ cup diced tomato
- ¼ cup sliced red onion
- 1 avocado, diced

Instructions:
1. In a glass bowl, mix the olive oil, maple seasoning, and lemon juice. Add the shrimp and toss. Keep chilled until you're ready to grill.
2. In a small mixing bowl, combine the olive oil, honey, lime juice, cilantro, balsamic vinegar, salt, and pepper. Set the vinaigrette aside.
3. Preheat either an indoor or outdoor medium-high grill.Serve the shrimp after threading them onto skewers. The shrimp should be grilled for about 2 minutes on each side, or until they are opaque and pink. Set aside the skewers after removing them.
4. Fill a large salad bowl halfway with mixed greens. Sliced cucumber, corn, tomato, red onion, and avocado should be placed on top of the greens. Place the grilled shrimp in the center of the salad. Drizzle the vinaigrette over the salad and toss to combine. Serve immediately.

Nutritional Info: Calories 443; Fat 24g; Sodium 1352mg; Carbs 32.7g; Fiber 8.8g; Sugar 19g; Protein 28g

Tabbouleh Salad

Preparation time: 15 minutes
Cooking time: 0 minutes
Servings: 4

Ingredients:
- ⅔ cup dry couscous
- 1 cup boiling water
- 1 small ripe tomato, diced
- 1 small green bell pepper, diced
- 1 shallot, finely diced
- ⅓ cup fresh parsley, chopped
- 1 garlic clove, minced
- Juice 1 fresh lemon
- 1 tbsp. olive oil
- ½ tsp. black pepper, freshly ground

Instructions:
1. In a small dish, combine the dried couscous. Within five minutes, combine the boiling water, cover, and set out. Put the parsley, tomato, green pepper, and onion in a salad bowl.
2. In a small bowl, combine the garlic, lemon juice, oil, and pepper. 3. In the salad dish, place the cooked couscous. Put the dressing on top and thoroughly combine by stirring.
3. Provide immediate delivery.

Nutritional Info: Calories: 120 kcal; Fat: 3 g; Carbs: 20 g; Protein: 3 g

Avocado, Tomato, And Olives Salad

Preparation time: 5 minutes
Cooking time: 0 minutes
Servings: 4

Ingredients
- 2 tbsp. olive oil
- 2 avocados, cut into wedges
- 1 cup Kalamata olives, pitted and halved
- 1 tbsp. balsamic vinegar
- 1 cup tomatoes, cubed
- 1 tbsp. ginger, grated
- Pinch black pepper
- 2 cups baby arugula

Instructions:
1. Combine the kalamata with the avocados and the other ingredients in a bowl, stir, and serve as a side dish.

Nutritional Info: Calories: 320 kcal; Fat: 30.4 g; Carbs: 13.9 g; Protein: 3 g

Radish And Olives Salad

Preparation time: 6 minutes
Cooking time: 0 minutes
Servings: 4

Ingredients
- 2 green onions, sliced
- 1-lb. radishes, cubed
- 2 tbsp. balsamic vinegar
- 2 tbsp. olive oil
- 1 tsp. chili powder
- 1 cup black olives, pitted and halved
- Pinch black pepper

Instructions:
1. In a large salad bowl, combine the potatoes, onions, and other ingredients. Toss with the remaining ingredients and serve as a side dish.

Nutritional Info: Calories: 123 kcal; Fat: 10.8 g; Carbs: 6.9 g; Protein: 1.3 g

Marinated Carrot and Celery Salad

Preparation time: 10 minutes plus 4 hours for refrigerating
Cooking time: 20 minutes
Serves: 4

Ingredients
- 2 pounds carrots, sliced
- 1 (10.75 ounces) can condensed tomato soup
- ¼ cup white sugar
- ½ cup white vinegar
- ¼ cup canola oil
- 1 teaspoon prepared mustard
- 1 teaspoon Worcestershire sauce
- ½ cup chopped celery
- ½ cup chopped green onion
- 1 green bell pepper, seeded and cut into strips

Instructions:
1. Boil a big pot of water, add the carrots, and cook for 3 to 5 minutes, or until soft. Drain, then put aside.
2. In a sizable mixing bowl, combine the soup, sugar, vinegar, oil, mustard, and Worcestershire sauce. Add the pepper, onion, celery, and carrots and toss to coat. To give the carrots time to marinate, put them in the fridge for at least 4 hours.

Nutritional Info: Calories 270; Fat 17g; Sodium 286mg; Carbs 28.5g; Fiber 8.7g; Sugar 15g; Protein 3.5g

Tomato Green Bean Soup

Preparation time: 15 minutes
Cooking time: 20 minutes
Servings: 9

Ingredients:
- 1 cup of chopped carrots
- Fresh basil: ¼ cup, chopped
- Oil: 2 tsp.
- Tomatoes: 3 cups, diced
- 1 minced garlic clove
- Vegetable broth: 6 cups, no-salt-added
- 1 cup of chopped onion
- Pepper: ¼ tsp.
- Green beans: 1 pound, 1-inch pieces

Instructions:
1. Saute carrots and onion in a pan with heated oil for 5 minutes.
2. Stir in the garlic, nuts, and beans. Add the broth after one minute of cooking.
3. Bring to a boil, then reduce to a low heat and cook for 20 minutes.
4. Add the peppers, tomatoes, and basil.
5. Simmer for 5 minutes, covered. Serve

Nutritional Info: Calories: 58 kcal; Fat: 1 g; Carbs: 10 g; Protein: 4 g

Potato-Fennel Soup

Preparation time: 15 minutes
Cooking time: 20 minutes
Servings: 8

Ingredients
- Olive oil: 1 tsp.
- Chopped red onion: 1 cup
- Lemon juice: 2 tsp.
- peeled russet potatoes, sliced
- Fennel bulb: 2 pounds, chopped
- Chicken broth: 3 cups, low-sodium
- Fennel seeds: 2 tsp., toasted
- Milk: 1 cup, non-fat

Instructions:
1. In a saucepan, sauté onion and fennel for 5 minutes in heated oil.
2. Stir in the milk, broth, potatoes, and lemon juice. 15 minutes of low-flame cooking.
3. Purée the soup using a stick blender in step 4. Top your serving with fennel seeds.

Nutritional Info: Calories: 149 kcal; Fat: 1.5 g; Carbs: 28 g; Protein: 6 g

Spinach And Endives Salad

Preparation time: 5 minutes
Cooking time: 0 minutes
Servings: 4

Ingredients
- 2 endives, roughly shredded
- 1 tbsp. dill, chopped
- ¼ cup lemon juice
- ¼ cup olive oil
- 2 cups baby spinach
- 2 tomatoes, cubed
- 1 cucumber, sliced
- ½ cups walnuts, chopped

Instructions:
1. In a large bowl, combine the endivos, spinach, and other ingredients. 2. Toss with the remaining ingredients and serve as a side dish.

Nutritional Info: Calories: 238 kcal; Fat: 22.3 g; Carbs: 8.5 g; Protein: 5.7 g

Radish and Tomato Salad

Preparation time: 8 minutes
Cooking time: None
Serves: 3 to 4

Ingredients
- 1 medium head romaine lettuce, torn
- 3 small tomatoes, diced
- 1 medium cucumber, sliced
- 1 small green bell pepper, sliced
- 1 small onion, cut into rings
- 6 radishes, thinly sliced
- ½ cup flat-leaf parsley, chopped
- ⅓ cup olive oil or avocado oil
- 3 tbsps lemon juice
- 1 garlic clove, minced
- Salt & pepper
- 1 teaspoon fresh mint, minced

Instructions:
1. In a salad bowl, combine the lettuce, tomatoes, cucumber, pepper, onion, radishes, and parsley.
2. Combine the olive oil, mint, lemon juice, garlic, salt, and pepper in a bowl.
3. Pour over the salad and coat well.

Nutritional Info: Calories 110; Fat 6.8g; Sodium 178mg; Carbs 11.6g; Fiber 4.5g; Sugar 5.6g; Protein 3g

Light Balsamic Salad

Preparation time: 9 minutes
Cooking time: 0 minutes
Servings: 3

Ingredients:
- 1 orange, cut into segments
- 2 green onions, chopped
- 1 romaine lettuce head, torn
- 1 avocado, pitted, peeled, and cubed
- ¼ cup almonds, sliced

For the Salad Dressing:
- 1 tsp. mustard
- ¼ cup olive oil
- 2 tbsp. balsamic vinegar
- Juice ½ orange
- Salt and black pepper

Instructions:
1. Combine the oranges, avocado, lettuce, almonds, and green onions in a salad dish.
2. Combine olive oil with vinegar, mustard, orange juice, salt, and pepper in a separate dish. Whisk well before adding the mixture to your salad and tossing to combine.

Nutritional Info: Calories: 35 kcal; Fat: 2 g; Carbs: 5 g; Protein: 0 g

Pesto Chicken & Cannellini Bean Soup

Preparation time: 15 minutes
Cooking time: 45 minutes
Servings: 8

Ingredients
- Chopped onion: 1 cup
- 2 cups of chicken broth, low-sodium
- Dried oregano: 1 tsp.
- Olive oil: 2 tbsp.
- Dried marjoram: 1 tsp.
- Chicken breasts: 2 pounds, skin removed & bone-in
- 1 can of (15 oz.) Cannellini beans, rinsed
- cups of sliced fennel
- Black pepper: half tsp.
- 3 minced garlic cloves
- Broccoli: 3 cups
- Chopped tomatoes: 2 cups
- Salt: ⅛ tsp.
- Pesto: ¼ cup

Instructions:
1. Cook garlic and onion for two to three minutes in hot oil.
2. Add the dry herbs and simmer for one minute. Add the chicken and broth, then cook it over high heat.
3. Cook for 20 to 22 minutes, or until the meat reaches an internal temperature of 165°F.
4. Remove the chicken and shred it.
5. Stir in the broccolini, fennel, tomatoes, and potatoes. For 4 to 10 minutes, simmer.
6. Stir in the beans, chicken, pepper, and salt. for three minutes.
7. Remove from the heat and stir in the pesto. Stir, then serve.

Nutritional Info: Calories: 270 kcal; Fat: 10 g; Carbs: 17 g; Protein: 26 g

Vegetable Weight-Loss Soup

Preparation time: 15 minutes
Cooking time: 35 minutes
Servings: 8

Ingredients
- 1 onion, chopped
- 2 minced garlic cloves
- 2 carrots, chopped
- 2 stalks celery, diced
- Green beans: 12 oz., half" pieces
- 4 cups of chopped kale
- Salt: ¼ tsp.
- Vegetable broth: 8 cups, low-sodium
- Olive oil: 2 tbsp.
- 2 cans of (15 oz.) Cannellini, rinsed & low-sodium
- Red-wine vinegar: 2 tsp.
- 2 zucchinis, diced
- Pesto: 8 tsp.
- 4 Roma tomatoes, chopped without seeds
- Pepper: half tsp.

Instructions:
1. Place oil over medium heat in a saucepan.
2. For ten minutes, sauté all vegetables in garlic.
3. Bring the broth to a boil. Reduce the heat and simmer for ten minutes.
4. Add the other ingredients, except the pasta, and increase the heat to high. For ten minutes, simmer.
5. Place pesto on top of the dish.

Nutritional Info: Calories: 225 kcal; Fat 8.4 g; Carbs: 6 g; Protein 12.7 g

Lemony Cucumber Salad

Preparation time: 4 minutes plus 2 to 3 hours for refrigerating
Cooking time: None
Serves: 2 to 3

Ingredients
- 2-3 cucumbers, sliced
- 2 tsp salt
- 3 tbsps lemon juice
- ¼ teaspoon paprika
- ¼ teaspoon white pepper
- ½ clove garlic, minced
- 4 fresh green onions, diced
- 1 cup thick Greek yogurt
- ¼ teaspoon paprika

Instructions:
1. Cut cucumbers into thin slices and toss with salt. Give yourself an hour to prepare.
2. Set aside a mixture of white pepper, garlic, paprika, lemon juice, and water. Slices of cucumber should be squeezed dry one at a time, then placed in the bowl. Eliminate and discard the liquid.
3. In a mixing bowl, combine the yogurt, green onions, and lemon juice. Combine everything, then sprinkle paprika or dill on top.
4. Place it in the refrigerator for a couple of hours.

Nutritional Info: Calories 212; Fat 1g; Sodium 1617mg; Carbs 41g; Fiber 5.4g; Sugar 27g; Protein 12g

Quinoa Cheese Salad

Preparation time: 8 minutes
Cooking time: None
Serves: 6

For the salad
- 2 cups cooked quinoa
- 2-3 cups frozen green peas
- ½ cup low-fat feta cheese
- 6 ounces pork, cubed
- ½ cup freshly chopped basil and cilantro
- ½ cup almonds, pulsed in a food processor until crushed

For the dressing
- ⅓ cup lemon juice (1-2 large juicy lemons)
- ⅓ cup olive oil or avocado oil
- ¼ teaspoon salt (more to taste)
- a few tsp lucuma powder to taste

Instructions:
1. Fill a saucepan halfway with water, bring to a boil, and then reduce to a low heat.
2. Cook the peas, covered, until they are bright green. Cook the pork in a skillet in the interim.
3. In a mixing dish, combine the quinoa, pork, peas, feta, herbs, and almonds. Utilizing a food processor, puree each component of the dressing.
4. Combine the dressing with the salad's components. To taste, add salt and pepper to the food.
5. Place baby spinach on the side and serve.

Nutritional Info: Calories 268; Fat 12.8g; Sodium 352mg; Carbs 23.7g; Fiber 4.4g; Sugar 5g; Protein 14.7g

Curried Carrot & Apple Soup

Preparation time: 15 minutes
Cooking time: 35 minutes
Servings: 4

Ingredients
- 1 onion, chopped
- 1 stick of celery, chopped
- Curry powder: 1 tbsp.
- 1 bay leaf
- Olive oil: 1 tbsp.
- 2 carrots, thinly sliced
- Broth: 4 cups, low-sodium
- 2 large peeled apples, chopped
- A pinch of salt

Instructions:
1. On medium heat, sauté the onion and celery for 8 to 12 minutes.
2. Add the carrots, bay leaf, curry powder, and a touch of salt. 3. Cook for 2 minutes.
3. Bring to a boil, then reduce to a low heat and cover for 20 to 25 minutes.
4. Remove the bay leaf and puree the soup using a stick blender.
5. Season with black pepper and serve.

Nutritional Info: Calories: 276 kcal; Fat; Carbs: 12g: 14 g; Protein: 7.1 g

Garden Vegetable Beef Soup

Preparation time: 15 minutes
Cooking time: 1 hour & 10 minutes
Servings: 8

Ingredients
- 1 onion, diced
- ¼ cup of tomato paste
- 3 minced garlic cloves
- Lean ground beef: 1 ½ pounds
- 3 celery ribs, diced
- 1 can of (~15 oz.) Diced tomatoes with liquid
- Julienned carrots: 10 oz.
- Pepper: ¼ tsp.
- Shredded cabbage: 1 ½ cups
- Cut green beans: half cup
- 1 zucchini, chopped
- Dried basil: 1 tsp.
- 2 cans of (~15 oz.) Beef broth, low-sodium
- Red potato: 5 oz., chopped
- Dried oregano: half tsp.

Instructions:
1. In a 6-quart saucepan, combine the garlic, beef, and onion and cook for 6 to 8 minutes. Drain.
2. Add the celery and carrots and cook for 6 to 8 minutes. Then stir in the tomato paste and cook for 1 minute.
3. Add the other ingredients. Bring to a boil, then reduce the heat and simmer, covered, for 35 to 45 minutes. Serve

Nutritional Info: Calories: 207 kcal; Fat: 7 g; Carbs: 14 g; Protein: 21 g

Carrot Soup

Preparation time: 10 minutes
Cooking time: 40 minutes
Servings: 6

Ingredients
- 10 carrots, sliced
- All-purpose flour: 3 tbsp.
- Black pepper: ¼ tsp.
- Sugar: 1 ½ tbsp.
- Fresh parsley: 2 tbsp., chopped
- 2 cups of water
- Ground nutmeg: ¼ tsp.
- Non-fat milk: 4 cups

Instructions:
1. Add water, sugar, and carrots to the pan in step
2. Cook for 20 minutes with the lid on. Save a little carrot water and discard the rest.
3. Heat the flour in a skillet over medium heat. Whisk together the milk, nutmeg, and pepper. Cook until it becomes thick.
4. In a blender, combine the white sauce and carrots and blend until smooth.
5. Add some preserved water, if necessary, to get the desired consistency.
6. Top the dish with fresh herbs.

Nutritional Info: Calories: 124 kcal; Fat: 17.2 g; Carbs: 24 g; Protein: 7 g

Lunch Recipes

Sesame Flatbread Pizza

Preparation time: 25 minutes
Cooking time: 1 hour 10 minutes
Serves: 5

Ingredients
- 2 tsp grapeseed oil
- 1 ½ cups flour
- 1 teaspoon onion powder:
- 2 tsp agave syrup
- 1 teaspoon oregano
- 2 tsp sesame seed
- 1 teaspoon sea salt

Instructions:
1. Preheat the oven to 400°F.
2. In a big bowl, combine the aforementioned ingredients and add about 12 cups of purified spring water. After that, gradually add water as you form the dough into balls. Apply a thin layer of grapeseed oil to the baking sheet. To effectively roll the dough onto the baking sheet, add flour to your hands.
3. Use a fork to poke holes into the top of the crust after brushing it with grapeseed oil. The crust should then be baked for at least 10 minutes. While you are waiting for the crust to cook, go ahead and make the pizza sauce. Add onions, pizza sauce, pepperoni, mushrooms, and Brazil nut cheese once the crust has fully baked. Afterward, bake your pizza for at least one hour. After that, serve and take pleasure.

Nutritional Info: Calories 169; Fat 2.8g; Sodium 469mg; Carbs 31.4g; Fiber 1.3g; Sugar 2.3g; Protein 4g

Tuna Bites with Walnuts

Preparation time: 15 minutes
Cooking time: None
Serves: 4

Ingredients
- ⅔ sheet nori
- 2 cups walnuts, chopped
- 4 key limes, juiced
- 2 Roma tomatoes
- ¼ teaspoon onion powder
- ¼ teaspoon dried oregano
- ¼ teaspoon ginger powder
- ¼ teaspoon dried thyme
- ¼ teaspoon sea salt
- ¼ teaspoon cayenne powder
- 2 tbsps coconut oil

the nori sheets:
1. To remove one-third of the nori sheets, fold them into three equal folds and cut along the first wrinkle.
2. Now place the pieces of the cut third of the nori sheet on top of one another, fold them in half, and cut along the crease.
3. Carry out step 3 with the remaining nori sheet, then add the bits to the food processor.

Prepare the tomatoes:
1. Remove the tops and cut each into five equal pieces.Then, cover the food processor with the lid, add the additional ingredients, and pulse for 3–4 minutes, until everything is completely combined and well blended.
2. Scoop out rough balls of the mixture and place them on a serving dish.

Nutritional Info: Calories 344; Fat 33g; Sodium 150mg; Carbs 12g; Fiber 3.7g; Sugar 3.4g; Protein 6.9g

Herbed Grain Burgers

Preparation time: 10 minutes
Cooking time: 15 minutes
Serves: 2

Ingredients
- ¼ cup bell peppers, finely diced
- 1 teaspoon oregano
- 1 teaspoon basil
- Sea salt and cayenne pepper
- ¼ onion, diced
- 1 ½ cups garbanzo bean flour
- 1 teaspoon dill
- 1 tbsp grapeseed oil
- 1 ½ cups cooked grains

Instructions:
1. Place the onions and pepper in a pan with a tbsp of grapeseed oil, and cook until tender.
2. Combine the other ingredients in a sizable bowl with the sautéed vegetables in step
3. Create patties with your fingers and cook them for about 4 minutes on each side, or until they are crispy.

Nutritional Info: Calories 833; Fat 19g; Sodium 49mg; Carbs 133g; Fiber 23g; Sugar 18g; Protein 38g

Mushroom-Pepper Tacos

Preparation time: 10 minutes
Cooking time: 12 minutes
Serves: 4

Ingredients
- 4 large Portobello mushrooms
- 2 medium red bell peppers, cored, sliced
- 4 medium green bell peppers, cored, sliced
- 2 medium white onions, peeled, sliced
- ⅔ teaspoon onion powder
- ⅔ teaspoon habanero seasoning
- ⅔ teaspoon cayenne pepper
- 1 key lime, juiced
- 2 tbsps grapeseed oil
- 2 medium avocados, peeled, pitted, sliced
- 8 tortillas, corn-free

Prepare the mushrooms:
1. First, slice the mushrooms into pieces that are each 13 inches thick after removing the stems and gills.
2. Heat a sizable skillet over medium heat, add 1 tbsp of oil, and when it is heated, add the onion and bell pepper. Cook, stirring occasionally, for 2 minutes, or until the vegetables are tender-crisp.
3. Add the sliced mushrooms, season with all the seasoning, toss to combine, and simmer for a further 7-8 minutes, or until the vegetables are tender. Warm up the tortillas as you wait.

Assemble the tacos
1. Spoon the cooked fajitas evenly into the center of each tortilla, top with avocado, and drizzle with lime juice. Serve straight away.

Nutritional Info: Calories 375; Fat 23g; Sodium 70mg; Carbs 41g; Fiber 12g; Sugar 6.8g; Protein 7g

Marinated Portobello Burgers

Preparation time: 4 minutes
Cooking time: 20 minutes
Serves: 4

Ingredients
- 4 large Portobello mushroom caps
- 2 large avocados; pitted, peeled, flesh sliced
- 2 medium tomatoes, sliced
- 2 cups purslane

Marinade:
- 2 tsp cayenne pepper
- 4 tsp dried basil
- 2 tsp dried oregano
- 1 teaspoon onion powder
- 6 tbsps olive oil

Prepare the mushrooms:
1. Slice each mushroom like a bun by first removing the stem and then cutting off about 12 inches of the top.

Prepare the marinade:
1. Place all the ingredients in a small bowl and whisk to thoroughly incorporate.
2. Place the prepared mushroom caps on a cookie sheet that has been lined with foil and greased with oil. Each mushroom cap should be filled with the marinade that has been prepared. After 10 minutes, let it rest.
3. In the interim, preheat the oven to 425 degrees. The mushroom caps should be baked for another 10 minutes, 10 on each side, until they are soft.
4. To serve, place the stuffed baked mushroom caps cap-side up on plates and evenly spread the avocado, tomato, and purslane within. Serve immediately.

Nutritional Info: Calories 364; Fat 35.4g; Sodium 22mg; Carbs 13.5g; Fiber 8g; Sugar 2.5g; Protein 3.5g

Curried Eggplant with Quinoa

Preparation time: 5 minutes
Cooking time: 5 minutes
Serves: 3

Ingredients
- 1 piece roasted eggplant
- juice of 1 lemon
- 1 teaspoon sea salt
- 1 teaspoon curry powder
- Water as required
- Cooked quinoa required for serving

Instructions:
1. Remove everything from the eggplant shell.
2. In a food processor, combine the eggplant, lemon juice, sesame oil, salt, and curry powder. Process the mixture until smooth. Put a small pot on the stove at medium heat.
3. Place your saucepan with the eggplant mixture in it and heat it slowly for about five minutes. If necessary, thin it with water. The quinoa is great over the curried eggplant!

Nutritional Info: Calories 77; Fat 0.7g; Sodium 1169mg; Carbs 18g; Fiber 8.8g; Sugar 10g; Protein 3g

Zoodles with Avocado Sauce

Preparation time: 10 minutes
Cooking time: 20 minutes
Serves: 4

Ingredients
- 4 large zucchinis, destemmed
- 4 avocados; pitted, peeled, sliced
- 4 cups basil leaves
- 48 cherry tomatoes, sliced
- 1 ½ teaspoon salt
- 1 cup walnuts, chopped
- 8 tbsps key lime juice
- 1 cup water

Instructions:
1. To prepare zucchini, cut off the ends of each one, then use a spiralizer or vegetable peeler to create noodles. Place it aside till required.
2. Add the avocado, basil, salt, and almonds to a blender. 3. Process the lime juice and water for 1-2 minutes on high, or until a thick sauce forms.
3. Place the zucchini noodles in a sizable bowl, add the sauce that has been thoroughly incorporated, add the tomatoes, and toss until the noodles are evenly coated. Serve immediately.

Nutritional Info: Calories 500; Fat 43g; Sodium 899mg; Carbs 31g; Fiber 17.6g; Sugar 7.7g; Protein 9g

Crusted Salmon and Asparagus with Almonds

Preparation time: 8 minutes
Cooking time: 15 minutes
Serves: 4

Almond herb mixture:
- ¼ cup ground almonds
- 1 tbsp fresh basil chopped, or dried
- 1 tbsp fresh parsley chopped, or dried
- 1 teaspoon fresh oregano, or dried
- salt & pepper to taste

Salmon & asparagus:
- ½ pound asparagus stalks
- 2 tbsps extra-virgin olive oil
- zest & juice from ½ lemon
- 4 6-ounce salmon fillets

Instructions:
1. Preparation in the oven: 400 °F
2. Combine the ground almonds, herbs, salt, and pepper in a small bowl. 4. Set aside for the time being.
3. Spread the asparagus on a baking sheet and brush the stale bread with oil. Season the asparagus with a pinch of sea salt and half of the lemon zest. To combine, toss everything together. To create room for the salmon, push the asparagus to the sides of the baking tray.
4. Spread the ahi fillets across the tray with the skin side down. Spoon the mixture of almonds and herbs evenly over the salmon pieces after squeezing the lemon juice over them. Add the remaining lemon zest and juice on top.
5. Roast the fish for 10 to 12 minutes at 400°F, or until it is thoroughly cooked.

Nutritional Info: Calories 659; Fat 11g; Sodium 10mg; Carbs 66g; Fiber 1.7g; Sugar 3.4g; Protein 85g

Stir-Fried Tofu and Green Beans

Preparation time: 10 minutes
Cooking time: 5 minutes
Serves: 4

Ingredients
- 1 pound firm tofu
- 3 medium-sized zucchinis
- 3 pieces tomatoes
- 1 piece red bell pepper
- 1 piece green bell pepper
- ½ pound green beans
- 1 to 1 ½ cup fresh coconut milk
- 2 tbsps cold-pressed extra-virgin olive oil
- sea salt as needed
- pepper as needed
- ½ tbsp curry powder
- ¼ tbsp of ginger
- fresh assorted selection of herbs

Instructions:
1. Cut the tofu into slices. Cut your zucchini into pieces. Cut the beans, tomatoes, and bell peppers into small pieces.
2. Pour oil into a pan and heat it over medium heat. Add the tofu and cook it for two to three minutes. Stir-fry the zucchini, beans, and bell pepper for two to three minutes. Cook for a bit after adding the tomatoes and coconut milk.
3. Season the dish with herbs, ginger, salt, and pepper. Serve with some soba noodles or wild rice.

Nutritional Info: Calories 402; Fat 31g; Sodium 35mg; Carbs 17g; Fiber 6.7g; Sugar 6g; Protein 21.5g

Southwest Tofu Scramble

Preparation time: 15 minutes
Cooking time: 15 minutes
Servings: 1

Ingredients:
- ½ tbsp olive oil
- ½ red onion, chopped
- 2 cups chopped spinach
- 8 ounces firm tofu, drained well
- 1 tsp ground cumin
- ½ tsp garlic powder
- Optional for serving: sliced avocado or sliced tomatoes

Instructions:
1. In a medium saucepan over medium heat, warm the olive oil. Place the onion in a pot and simmer for five minutes. Add the spinach and cover; let it simmer for two minutes.
2. Using a spatula, move the vegetables to one side of the pan. With a fork, crumble the tofu into the open space in the pan. Mix well after adding the cumin and garlic to the crumbled tofu. Cook the tofu for 5 to 7 minutes, or until it begins to colour slightly.
3. Serve immediately with whole-wheat bread, fruit, or nuts. Optionally, top with sliced avocado and tomato.

Nutritional Info: Calories: 267 kcal; Fat: 17 g; Carbs: 13 g; Protein: 23 g

Awesome Zucchini Hummus Wrap

Preparation time: 15 minutes
Cooking time: 10 minutes
Serves: 4

Ingredients
- ½ medium red onion; peeled, sliced
- 2 medium plum tomatoes, sliced
- 2 cups romaine lettuce, chopped
- 2 large zucchinis
- ½ teaspoon sea salt
- ½ teaspoon cayenne pepper
- 2 tbsps grapeseed oil
- 4 spelt flour tortillas
- 8 tbsps hummus, homemade

Instructions:
1. Rinse the zucchini, trim the ends, and cut it into slices. Next, prepare a grill pan over medium heat while liberally greasing it with oil.
2. In the meantime, place the zucchini slices in a medium basin, add the oil, salt, and cayenne pepper, and toss to evenly coat.
3. Arrange the zucchini slices on the hot grill pan. Cook for 3 minutes or until they are golden brown, then flip them over and cook for an additional 2 minutes. Place it aside till required.

Heat the tortillas:
1. Place them on the grill pan and cook for 1 minute on each side, or until the bread is hot and has grill markings.

Assemble the wraps:
1. Spread 2 tbsps of hummus on one side of each tortilla, top with one-fourth of the zucchini pieces, one-half cup of lettuce, and one-fourth of the tomato slices, working on one wrap at a time. Repeat with the remaining tortillas, wrap them securely, and serve.

Nutritional Info: Calories 278; Fat 12g; Sodium 703mg; Carbs 36.7g; Fiber 3g; Sugar 7g; Protein 5.8g

Apple and Celery with Almonds

Preparation time: 60 minutes
Cooking time: None
Serves: 2

Ingredients
- 10 ounces sliced up knob celery
- 6-7 ounces cubed up apples
- 2 or 3 cups water
- ⅓ cup almonds
- ½ lemon
- ½ tbsp salt
- Pepper as needed

Instructions:
1. Place the apples, celery, and lemon juice in a medium bowl. Mix everything thoroughly. To make an exceptionally excellent and smooth paste, pulse your almonds in a blender with a little water.
2. Place the paste in a bowl and season with salt and pepper to taste. Blend well and let it sit for 60 minutes.
3. Stir the paste into the bowl with the apples before serving.

Nutritional Info: Calories 83; Fat 0.6g; Sodium 1865mg; Carbs 20g; Fiber 5g; Sugar 13g; Protein 1.7g

Spicy Shrimp Stir Fry

Preparation time: 15 minutes
Cooking time: 30 minutes
Serves: 5

Spicy Aioli:
- ½ cup homemade mayo or purchased paleo mayo
- 1 clove garlic, minced
- 1 teaspoon sesame oil
- 1 ½ tsp lime juice or lemon juice
- 2 to 3 tsp hot sauce 30-day-whole-food – compliant
- Pinch cayenne pepper or to taste

Shrimp Stir Fry:
- 1 pound shrimp peeled
- 2 tbsps coconut oil
- Sea salt and pepper for shrimp*
- 6 cups slaw mix or a combination of shredded cabbage, carrots, brussels sprouts, etc.
- 3 tbsps coconut aminos
- 2 tbsps sesame oil
- 1 teaspoon hot sauce 30-day-whole-food compliant, optional
- 1 bunch scallions thinly sliced white or light green and green parts separated
- 3 cloves garlic minced
- 2 tsp ginger fresh, about 1" peeled and grated or minced

To prepare the Aioli:
1. Combine the mayo, garlic, sesame oil, lime or lemon juice, spicy sauce, and cayenne, if using, in a bowl and whisk until smooth. Store it in the refrigerator until ready to use.

Stir Fry the Shrimp and Veggies:
1. Gather all of the ingredients and have them ready to go before you begin cooking because it will be quick.
2. Melt one tbsp of coconut oil in a large non-stick skillet or wok over high heat. If desired, season the shrimp with salt, pepper, and a dash of cayenne pepper.
3. Add the shrimp in a single layer after the skillet has started to smoke. Cook for about 2 minutes, turning once or twice, or until opaque. Put them on a plate and cover them while you cook the vegetables.
4. Reduce the heat to medium and stir in the final tbsp of coconut oil. When the slaw or shredded vegetables start to soften, add them along with the white pepper, ginger, and garlic. Cook and stir for approximately a minute.
5. Add the coconut aminos, the same oil, and hot sauce, if using, to the skillet and stir. Lower the heat and add the shrimp back in, stirring to thoroughly blend. Remove from the heat and garnish with the green onion.
6. Serve in dishes and top with hot aioli.

Nutritional Info: Calories 406; Fat 21.7g; Sodium 762mg; Carbs 42g; Fiber 4.3g; Sugar 9.6g; Protein 13.6g

Superb Lemon Roasted Artichokes

Preparation time: 10 minutes
Cooking time: 7 minutes
Servings: 2

Ingredients
- 3 peeled and sliced garlic cloves
- 2 lemon pieces
- 1 tsp Black pepper
- 4 artichoke pieces
- 1 tbsp. olive oil
- 1 tsp Sea flavored vinegar

Instructions:
1. Wash your artichokes well, dunk them in water, and trim the stems to be about ½ inch long. Trim the outer leaves and prickly points, then put lemon juice on the chokes. Place a trivet in the Instant Pot, poke garlic slivers between the choke leaves, and then add artichokes.
2. Lock the cover and cook for 7 minutes on high pressure.
3. Allow the pressure to naturally drop over ten minutes.
4. Transfer the artichokes to a chopping board, let them cool, then cut them in half lengthwise and slice the purple and white center.
5. Preheat the oven to 400°F.
6. Take a basin and stir. half a lemon and olive oil
7. Pour over the chopped halves and season with pepper and flavor-infused vinegar.
8. Heat an iron skillet in the oven for five minutes.
9. Add a few tsp of oil, then arrange the marinated artichoke halves in the skillet.
10. Brush with a mixture of lemon and olive oil.
11. Quarter the third lemon and nestle it between the halves.
12. Roast the chokes for 20 to 25 minutes, or until they are browned.
13. Serve and enjoy yourself!

Nutritional Info: Calories: 263 kcal; Fat: 16 g; Carbs: 8 g; Protein: 23 g

Thai Seafood Soup

Preparation time: 20 minutes
Cooking time: 40 minutes
Serves: 8

Ingredients
- 2 tbsps fat (ghee, olive oil)
- 4 cups bone broth (any kind you like)
- 3 tbsps cashew butter (or 1 cup cashew creamer or sup coconut cream for AIP)
- 3 pounds white fish filet (no scales or bones)
- 2 bay leaves
- 1 large Vidalia onion
- 2 inch nub of ginger
- 4 garlic cloves
- 3 carrots
- 2 teaspoon salt
- 4 baby bok choy
- 2 cans water chestnuts
- 3 lemons
- **To taste:**
- 2 tbsps fish sauce, as you like to taste
- 1 bunch cilantro
- 2 tbsps wasabi powder

Instructions:
1. Melt two tbsps of fat in a large stockpot over medium heat.
2. Finely chop the ginger, onions, carrots, garlic, and other ingredients.
3. After the pot has heated, add the diced vegetables and bay leaf.
4. Cook, sometimes stirring, for about 8 minutes, until tender.
5. In the meantime, chop, wash, and take apart your bok choi while cutting the fish into 1-inch pieces.
6. Peel a few triangular pieces of lemon rind and add them to the pot. 7.
7. Add the fish to the pot and thoroughly stir it to cook all of the fish.
8. Add the salt, the cashew cream, the fish sauce, and the waab powder. Mix well.
9. Stir in the broth, and let it boil for 10 minutes.
10. Include the water chestnuts and the bok choy. Stir. Bring it to the summer.
11. Juice all of the lemons. Place aside.
12. Leave the soup to simmer for an additional 10 minutes.
13. Slice your cucumber.
14. Include the lemon juice. Stir. Taste and adjust the salt as needed. Add some water if you want it to be thinner.
15. Garnish with plenty of fresh cilantro!

Nutritional Info: Calories 532; Fat 27g; Sodium 2431mg; Carbs 30.4g; Fiber 6.4g; Sugar 9g; Protein 45g

Shrimp and Zoodles

Preparation time: 4 minutes
Cooking time: 20 minutes
Serves: 3 to 4

Ingredients
- 3 cloves garlic, crushed
- 3 tbsps olive oil or avocado oil divided
- 1 pound raw shrimp peeled deveined
- Juice of 1 lemon
- 1 teaspoon lemon zest
- ¼ cup chicken broth
- 3 tbsps ghee
- 3 tbsps fresh chopped parsley
- Salt and pepper to taste
- 2 large zucchini

Instructions:
1. To begin, combine 1 tbsp of oil and 1 clove of garlic. The shrimp should be coated and left to marinade for 30 minutes. (Optional, but increases the shrimp's flavor.)
2. In a big sauce pan, heat the final 2 tbsps of oil. The shrimp won't be completely cooked after being added and cooking for 1-2 minutes on each side. Keep the oil in the pan and set it aside. Keep the pan heated.
3. Cook for one minute, or until the last of the garlic is fragrant. Lemon juice, chicken broth, and zest are added. Cook for a further three minutes to reduce the sauce.
4. Fill the pan with butter. Cook for a further three minutes, or until the sauce starts to thicken.
5. Add the shrimp back to the pan and cook for an additional 2 minutes on each side, covering them with the sauce as you go.
6. Before making the zucchini noodles, spiralize the zucchini. Add about 1 tbsp of oil, then either bake at 375 degrees for 10 minutes or sauté in oil for five minutes. You can also serve raw food.
7. zucchini and shrimp in a sauce. To serve, garnish with fresh parsley.

Nutritional Info: Calories 319; Fat 21g; Sodium 1062mg; Carbs 8g; Fiber 2g; Sugar 5g; Protein 26g

Mushroom-Tomato Pasta

Preparation time: 25 minutes
Cooking time: 1 hour
Serves: 4

Ingredients
- 2 packs enoki mushrooms, about 400 grams total
- 8 round slices butternut squash, fresh
- 3 medium white onions, peeled, sliced
- 4 medium bell peppers, cored, sliced
- 2 cups cherry tomatoes
- 1 ½ tsp sea salt
- 4 tbsps coconut oil

Instructions:
1. Peal the eight slices of butternut squash, then cut out the seeds. When the water in a big pot is halfway filled, add the butternut squash and bring the mixture to a boil over medium-high heat.
2. When the potatoes are soft, drain any remaining cooking liquid and mash them with a fork. Place the mushrooms, onion, and bell pepper in the saucepan and simmer for 15 to 20 minutes, or until the mushrooms are soft.
3. Add salt. Turn off the heat. Allow the mixture to cool for 15 minutes.
4. Stir thoroughly after adding the coconut oil and letting it melt.
5. Distribute the spaghetti equally among the four plates, then serve with cherry tomatoes on top.

Nutritional Info: Calories 192; Fat 14g; Sodium 883mg; Carbs 16g; Fiber 4.6g; Sugar 5g; Protein 4.5g

Peppered Kale

Preparation time: 5 minutes
Cooking time: 15 minutes
Serves: 4

Ingredients
- ¼ cup white onion, diced
- 1 bunch of kale, fresh
- ¼ cup red pepper, diced
- ¼ teaspoon sea salt
- 1 teaspoon crushed red pepper
- 2 tbsps grapeseed oil

Prepare the kale:
1. Thoroughly rinse it. Cut the leaves into bite-sized pieces and take off the stem.
2. Drain thoroughly with a salad spinner.
3. Preheat a large skillet over high heat. Add the oil, then when it is heated, add the onion and red pepper. Season with salt and cook for 3 minutes, or until the vegetables are starting to get soft.
4. Reduce heat to low. Add the kale leaves. Toss to combine. Then cover the skillet with a lid and cook for an additional five minutes.
5. Add the red pepper to the kale, toss to combine, put the cover back on the skillet, and simmer for an additional 3 minutes, or until the vegetables are soft. Serve immediately.

Nutritional Info: Calories 74; Fat 7g; Sodium 153mg; Carbs 2.7g; Fiber 0.9g; Sugar 1g; Protein 1g

Chocolate Aquafaba Mousse

Preparation time: 20 minutes
Cooking time: 0 minutes
Servings: 4-6

Ingredients
- 1 tsp. pure vanilla extract
- 15 oz. unsalted chickpeas
- Fresh raspberries
- ¼ tsp. tartar cream
- 4 oz. dairy-free dark chocolate
- 1 tbsp. coconut sugar
- ¼ tsp. sea salt

Instructions:
1. Break up the dark chocolate into coarse pieces, then put it in a glass dish and heat it in a double boiler or over boiling water on the stovetop.
2. Gently melt the chocolate, stirring constantly, until completely melted.
3. Take the melted chocolate off the heat and pour it into a large mixing bowl.
4. Drain the chickpeas, reserving the brine (aqafaba), and store them for a different recipe, such as hummus.
5. Mix in the tartar cream with the aquafaba.
6. Using an electric hand mixer, combine the ingredients on high speed for 7 to 10 minutes, or until soft peaks start to form.
7. Combine the salt, vanilla extract, and coconut sugar in a mixing bowl. Then, thoroughly combine the mixture.
Add half of the melted chocolate to the whisked acai bowl and mix until combined.
9. To make the mousse, fold in the remaining aquafaba until it is well combined and smooth.
10. Gently spoon the chocolate mousse into ramekins, small Mason jars, or glasses.
11. Cover with cling film and refrigerate for no less than three hours.
12. Scatter raspberries over the mousse and serve.

Nutritional Info: Calories: 280 kcal; Fat: 13.8 g; Carbs: 34.7 g; Protein: 3.9 g

Grilled Chicken Cobb Salad

Preparation time: 4 minutes
Cooking time: 20 minutes
Serves: 6

Ingredients
- 4 bacon pieces, diced
- 2 boneless, skinless chicken breasts, thinly sliced
- 3 tbsps barbecue sauce, or more to taste
- 2 hefty eggs
- 6 cups romaine lettuce, chopped
- 2 diced Roma tomatoes
- 1 halved, seeded, peeled, and diced avocado
- 1 cup drained canned corn kernels
- 1 cup drained and rinsed canned black beans

Dressing for the buttermilk ranch:
- 1 tbsp buttermilk
- ¼ cup unsweetened Greek yogurt
- 1 tbsp sour cream
- ½ teaspoon dill, dried
- ½ teaspoon parsley, dry
- ¼ teaspoon powdered garlic
- Freshly ground black pepper, to taste
- Salt and pepper, to taste

Instructions:
1. Combine buttermilk, Greek yogurt, sour cream, parsley, dill, garlic powder, salt, and pepper in a small bowl.
2. In a big skillet over medium heat, pour in the oil. Cook for 6 to 8 minutes, or until the bacon is brown and crispy. Then, move it to a dish that has been lined with paper towels and put it aside.
3. Season the chicken breasts with salt and pepper to taste. Cook, turning once, for 3-4 minutes per side, or until thoroughly cooked. Slice it into bite-sized pieces after it has fully cooled.
4. Combine the chicken and BBQ sauce in a medium bowl by gently tossing the ingredients.
5. Put the eggs in a big pot and pour 1 inch of cold water over them. Bring to a boil, then simmer for one minute on low heat. Eggs should be taken off the heat, covered with a tight-fitting lid, and left for 8 to 10 minutes. Drain and cool thoroughly before peeling and dicing.
6. To make the salad, layer rows of bacon, BBQ chicken, eggs, tomatoes, avocado, corn, and beans on top of romaine lettuce in a large bowl.
7. Garnish with buttermilk ranch dressing and serve immediately.

Nutritional Info: Calories 285; Fat 10.7g; Sodium 218mg; Carbs 23.3g; Fiber 7g; Sugar 6g; Protein 26g

Aromatic Salmon With Fennel Seeds

Preparation time: 8 minutes
Cooking time: 10 minutes
Servings: 2

Ingredients
- 2 medium salmon fillets, skinless and boneless
- 1 tbsp. fennel seeds
- 2 tbsp. olive oil
- 1 tbsp. lemon juice
- 1 tbsp. water

Instructions:
1. Olive oil has to be heated on a stove.
2. Add funnel seeds to the pan and toast for 1 minute.
Add salmon fillets and lemon juice to the pan in step
4. Add water and cook the fish for four minutes on each side over medium heat.

Nutritional Info: Calories: 301 kcal; Fat: 18.2 g; Carbs: 0.8 g; Protein: 4.8 g

The OG Tuna Sandwich

Preparation time: 15 minutes
Cooking time: 5 minutes
Servings: 2

Ingredients
- 30 g olive oil
- 1 medium cucumber, peeled and diced
- ½ g pepper
- 4 whole-wheat bread slices
- 85 g onion, diced
- ½ g salt
- 1 can flavored tuna
- 85 g spinach, shredded

Instructions:
1. Spinach, tuna, onion, oil, salt, and pepper should all be added to a blender and pulsed for around 10 to 20 seconds.
2. While preparing the tuna mixture, toast your bread and add your diced cucumber to a bowl. Carefully combine and add the mixture to the bread after it has been toasted.
3. Cut in half and serve with the remaining mixture refrigerated.

Nutritional Info: Calories: 302 kcal; Fat: 5.8 g; Carbs: 36.62 g; Protein: 28 g

Worcestershire Pork Chops

Preparation time: 15 minutes
Cooking time: 15 Minutes
Servings: 3

Ingredients
- 2 tbsps Worcestershire sauce
- 4 oz pork loin chops
- 1 tbsp lemon juice
- 1 tsp olive oil

Instructions:
1. Combine the Worcestershire sauce, lemon juice, and extra virgin olive oil in a mixing bowl. Apply the sauce mixture to the pork loin chops on each side. Heat the grill to 395 degrees.
2. Cook the pork chops for 5 minutes on each side on a hot grill. Then turn the pork chops over and coat them with the remaining sauce mixture. Grill the meat for a further 7 to 8 minutes.

Nutritional Info: Calories: 267 kcal; Fat: 20.4 g; Carbs: 2.1 g; Protein: 17g

Greek Pork

Preparation time: 15 minutes
Cooking time: 50 Minutes
Servings: 8

Ingredients
- lb. Pork roast, sliced into cubes
- ¼ cup chicken broth
- ¼ cup lemon juice
- 2 tsps dried oregano
- 2 tsps garlic powder

Instructions:
1. Place the meat in the pressure cooker. Combine all the remaining ingredients in a large bowl. Apply the mixture to the meat. Throw to the side only. Protect the pot.
2. Select "manual" mode. 50 minutes of high-pressure cooking natural pressure release.

Nutritional Info: Calories 478 kcal; Fat: 21.6 g; Carbs: 1.2 g; Protein 65.1g

Potato, Parsley, and Pumpkin Patties

Preparation time: 10 minutes
Cooking time: 5 minutes
Serves: 2

Ingredients
- 1 pound pumpkin
- 1 pound potatoes
- 2 ½ ounces soy flour
- 4 tbsps water
- 3 tbsps chopped up parsley
- sea salt as needed
- organic salt as needed
- a pinch of pepper
- cold pressed extra-virgin olive oil

Instructions:
1. Remove the skins from the potatoes and pumpkin. Both of them should be grated into large pieces using a grater.
2. Put 2 tsp of soy flour and 4 tbsps of water in a bowl.
3. In a separate bowl, combine the soy flour with the grated pumpkin and potatoes. Flour the mixture, then thoroughly combine it. Add some pepper, parsley, and salt to taste.
4. Set a pan over a medium heat source. Heat it up and add oil. Make patties from the mixture and cook them for a couple of minutes in hot oil until they are browned.

Nutritional Info: Calories 399; Fat 7.8g; Sodium 26mg; Carbs 69g; Fiber 10g; Sugar 12g; Protein 19.7g

Pork With Green Beans & Potatoes

Preparation time: 15 minutes
Cooking time: 22 Minutes
Servings: 6

Ingredients
- 1 lb. Lean pork, sliced into cubes
- 1 onion, chopped
- 2 carrots, sliced thinly
- 2 cups canned crushed tomatoes
- 4 potatoes, cubed

Instructions:
1. Set the Instant Pot to sauté in step 1. Incorporate ½ cup of olive oil. During the five minutes of cooking, toss the meat often. Add the remaining ingredients. Mix well.
2. Close the pot. Select the manual setting. Cook for 17 minutes at high pressure. natural pressure release.

Nutritional Info: Calories: 428 kcal; Fat: 24.4 g; Carbs: 27.6 g; Protein: 26.7g

Salmon And Beans Mix

Preparation time: 10 minutes
Cooking time: 20 minutes
Servings: 4

Ingredients
- 2 tbsp. coconut aminos
- ½ cup olive oil
- 1 and ½ cup low-sodium chicken stock
- 4 oz. salmon fillets
- 4 garlic cloves, minced
- 1 tbsp. ginger, grated
- 1 cup black beans, canned, no-salt-added, drained, and rinsed
- 1 tsp. balsamic vinegar
- ¼ cup radishes, grated
- ¼ cup carrots, grated
- ¼ cup scallions, chopped

Instructions:
1. In a bowl, mix together the aminos and half of the oil.
2. Arrange the salmon in a baking dish, top with the coconut aminos and stock, and bake for 10 minutes. Then, place the baking dish under a preheated broiler and cook for 4 minutes on each side.
3. Heat a pan with the remaining oil over medium heat. Add the garlic, ginger, and black beans, and stir. Cook for three minutes.
4. Stir in the vinegar, potatoes, carrots, and onions, and cook for another five minutes.
5. Divide the fish and the black bean mixture among the plates and serve them.
6. Enjoy!

Nutritional Info: Calories: 220 kcal; Fat: 4 g; Carbs: 12 g; Protein: 7 g

Beef & Potatoes

Preparation time: 15 minutes
Cooking time: 20 minutes
Servings: 6

Ingredients
- 1 ½ lb. Stew beef, sliced into cubes
- 2 tsps mixed dried herbs (thyme, sage)
- potatoes, cubed
- 10 oz. Mushrooms
- 1 ½ cups red wine

Instructions:
1. Set the Instant Pot to sauté in step 1. Add one tbsp of olive oil before browning the beef all over. Add the remaining ingredients.
2. Season with pepper and salt to taste. Add 1 ½ cups of water to the saucepan. Mix well. Protect the pot. Set it to automatic. Cook for 20 minutes at high pressure. natural pressure release.

Nutritional Info: Calories: 360 kcal; Fat: 9.6g; Carbs: 29.3 g; Protein: 29.9g

Fried Rice with Veggies

Preparation time: 20 minutes
Cooking time: 60 minutes
Serves: 2

Ingredients
- ½ cup sliced zucchini
- 1 tbsp grapeseed oil
- ½ cup sliced mushrooms
- ¼ cubed onions
- ½ cup sliced bell pepper
- 1 cup cooked quinoa
- cayenne pepper and sea salt to your taste

Instructions:
1. Saute the onion until it is properly fried in a pan with hot grapeseed oil. Place the vegetables in and give them at least 6 minutes to cool. Make sure the vegetables don't simmer for too long or go mushy.
2. 1 cup of cooked quinoa or wild rice should be added next. Cook until a light brown color appears. After that, serve and take pleasure.

Nutritional Info: Calories 202; Fat 8.8g; Sodium 13mg; Carbs 26.7g; Fiber 3.7g; Sugar 5g; Protein 5.7g

Black-Eyed Peas And Greens Power Salad

Preparation time: 15 minutes
Cooking time: 6 minutes
Servings: 2

Ingredients
- 1 tbsp olive oil
- 3 cups purple cabbage, chopped
- 5 cups baby spinach
- 1 cup shredded carrots
- 1 can black-eyed peas, drained
- Juice of ½ lemon
- Pinch Salt
- 1 tsp freshly ground black pepper

Instructions:
1. Heat the oil and cabbage in a medium saucepan over medium heat for 1 to 2 minutes.
2. Cover and cook for three to four minutes over medium heat, or until the spinach is wilted. Remove it from the heat and pour it into a large basin.
3. Stir in the carrots, black-eyed peas, and lemon juice. When seasoning, add salt and pepper if desired. Throw and serve.

Nutritional Info: Calories: 320 kcal; Fat: 9 g; Carbs: 49 g; Protein: 16 g

Rosemary Salmon

Preparation time: 8 minutes
Cooking time: 15 minutes
Serves: 3

Ingredients
- 2 wild caught sockeye salmon filets, 10 ounces total
- 1 teaspoon salt
- 2 tablespoons ghee
- 1 tbsp minced garlic, about 2-3 cloves
- 1 tablespoon chopped fresh rosemary
- zest of 1 orange
- juice of 2 oranges, about ⅓ cup
- 1 teaspoon tapioca starch

Instructions:
1. Preheat the oven to 425°F and prepare a baking sheet with parchment paper.
2. Season each filet with ½ teaspoon salt and bake for 6 to 8 minutes.
3. While the salmon bakes, combine the butter and garlic in a sauce pan and heat over medium heat for about three minutes.
4. Include the rosemary, orange zest, and orange juice. Cook for a further three minutes.
5. Make sure to thoroughly mix in the tapioca starch so that there are no lumps left. Turn off the heat after stirring until just slightly thickened.
6. Remove the ham from the oven, plate it, and drizzle some garlic-orange sauce on top.

Nutritional Info: Calories 146; Fat 7g; Sodium 890mg; Carbs 4.8g; Fiber 0.6g; Sugar 1.8g; Protein 15g

Black-Bean Soup

Preparation time: 15 minutes
Cooking time: 20 minutes
Servings: 4

Ingredients
- 1 yellow onion
- 1 tbsp olive oil
- 2 cans black beans, drained
- 1 cup diced fresh tomatoes
- 5 cups low-sodium vegetable broth
- ¼ tsp freshly ground black pepper
- ¼ cup chopped fresh cilantro

Instructions:
1. In a large sauté pan, sauté the onion in the olive oil for 4 to 5 minutes over medium heat.
2. Put the black beans, tomatoes, vegetable broth, and black pepper in Step 2. Within 15 minutes, bring it to a boil, then adjust the heat to simmer.
3. Remove the bay leaf, then add the soup to a blender and process until somewhat smooth, working in batches.
4. Place it back in the saucepan, add the cilantro, and heat through. Serve immediately.

Nutritional Info: Calories: 234 kcal; Fat: 5 g; Carbs: 37 g; Protein: 11 g

Simple Hummus

Preparation time: 35 minutes
Cooking time: 60 minutes
Serves: 7

Ingredients
- ⅓ cup homemade tahini butter
- onion powder
- 2 tbsps olive oil
- sea salt to your taste
- 2 tbsps key lime juice
- 1 cup cooked chickpeas

Instructions:
1. In a food processor, combine all of the ingredients listed above. After that, serve and take pleasure.

Nutritional Info: Calories 150; Fat 13g; Sodium 71mg; Carbs 6.8g; Fiber 1.8g; Sugar 1.2g; Protein 2g

Pork And Chestnuts Mix

Preparation time: 15 minutes
Cooking time: 0 minutes
Servings: 6

Ingredients
- 1 and ½ cups brown rice, already cooked
- 4 cups pork roast, already cooked and shredded
- 4 ounces water chestnuts, drained and sliced
- ½ cup sour cream
- A pinch of salt and white pepper

Instructions:
1. Combine the rice with the meat and the other ingredients in a large dish. Toss, then place in the refrigerator for two hours before serving.

Nutritional Info: Calories: 294 kcal; Fat: 17 g; Carbs: 16 g; Protein: 23.5g

Spicy Ginger Seabass

Preparation time: 5 minutes
Cooking time: 10 minutes
Servings: 2

Ingredients
- 1 tbsp. ginger, grated
- 2 tbsp. sesame oil
- ¼ tsp. chili powder
- 2 sea bass fillets, boneless
- 1 tbsp. margarine

Instructions:
1. In a skillet, warm the butter and sesame oil.
2. Ginger and chili powder are added.
3. The seafood has to cook for three minutes on each side after being added to the pan.
4. After that, cover the pan and simmer the fish for three minutes over low heat.

Nutritional Info: Calories: 216 kcal; Protein: 24 g; Carbs: 1.1 g; Fat: 12.3 g

Baked Potatoes And "BBQ" Lentils

Preparation time: 5 minutes
Cooking time: 10 minutes
Servings: 4

Ingredients:
- 4 sliced large baked potatoes
- 1 cup dry brown lentils
- 1 tsp. molasses
- 1 chopped small onion
- 1 tsp. liquid smoke
- 1 cup water
- ½ cup organic ketchup

Instructions:
1. Fill the pot with water, an onion, and lentils.
2. Cook for 10 minutes on high pressure with the lid closed.
3. Let the pressure drop naturally.
4. Add mustard, liquid smoke, and ketchup to the lentils.
5. Simmer for five minutes.
6. Serve the baked potatoes and enjoy them!

Nutritional Info: Calories: 140 kcal; Fat: 4 g; Carbs: 24 g; Protein: 5 g

Beef And Chili Mix

Preparation time: 15 minutes
Cooking time: 16 Minutes
Servings: 4

Ingredients
- 2 green chili peppers
- 2 oz beef flank steak
- 1 tsp salt
- 2 tbsps olive oil
- 1 tsp apple cider vinegar

Instructions:
1. Fill the skillet with olive oil. Place the flannels in the oil and roast them for three minutes on each side. Then sprinkle salt and apple cider vinegar over the cooked meat.
2. Finely chop the chile peppers and add them to the mixture. Fry the beef for 10 more minutes. From time to time, stir it.

Nutritional Info: Calories: 166 kcal; Fat: 10.5 g; Carbs: 0.2 g; Protein: 17.2 g

White Beans With Spinach And Pan-Roasted Tomatoes

Preparation time: 15 minutes
Cooking time: 10 minutes
Servings: 2

Ingredients
- 1 tbsp olive oil
- 4 small plum tomatoes, halved lengthwise
- 10 ounces frozen spinach, defrosted and squeezed of excess water
- 2 garlic cloves, thinly sliced
- 2 tbsps water
- ¼ tsp freshly ground black pepper
- 1 can white beans, drained
- Juice of 1 lemon

Instructions:
1. Heat the oil in a large pan over medium-high heat.2. The tomatoes should be cooked cut-side down for 3 to 5 minutes, then turned over and cooked for an additional minute. Send it to a place.
2. Reduce the heat to medium before adding the spinach, garlic, water, and pepper to the skillet.3. Cook, stirring for two to three minutes, or until the spinach is well heated.
3. Add the white beans and lemon juice to the skillet with the tomatillos and mix for 1 to 2 minutes until heated through.

Nutritional Info: Calories: 293 kcal; Fat: 9 g; Carbs: 43 g; Protein: 15 g

Dinner Recipes

Spicy Chicken Nuggets

Preparation time: 8 minutes
Cooking time: 20 minutes
Serves: 8

Ingredients
- 1 cup all-purpose flour
- 4 tsp seasoned salt
- 1 teaspoon poultry seasoning
- 1 teaspoon ground mustard
- 1 teaspoon paprika
- ½ teaspoon pepper
- 2 pounds boneless and skinless chicken breasts
- ¼ cup canola oil

Instructions:
1. In a large shallow dish, combine the first six ingredients. Chicken should be flattened to a thickness of 12 inches before being cut into 12 inch chunks. A few pieces of chicken at a time, placed on a platter, and tossed with sauce.
2. Fry the chicken in the canola oil in a skillet over medium-high heat until it forms a crust.
3. Dish out and savor!

Nutritional Info: Calories 260; Fat 10g; Sodium 634mg; Carbs 13g; Fiber 1g; Sugar 0.3g; Protein 27g

Dijon Salmon

Preparation time: 10 minutes
Cooking time: 15 minutes
Serves: 3

Ingredients
- 5 tbsps low-fat plain Greek yogurt
- 2 tbsps Dijon mustard
- 2 tsp worth of chopped fresh dill
- 4 fresh garlic cloves, minced
- 4 tbsps fresh lemon juice, freshly squeezed
- ½chili powder, to taste
- 4 5-ounce salmon fillets

Instructions:
1. Turn on the broiler and get it ready.
2. Combine the Greek yogurt, mustard, dill, garlic, lemon juice, and chili powder in a small bowl and stir to combine. 3.
3. Arrange the salmon fillets on the broiler pan in a single layer and spray with Pam cooking spray. 4. Broil the pan in the oven.
4. Place the salmon on a rack that is three inches away from the heat source of the broiler after coating it with the sauce.
5. Place it for 5 to 6 minutes under the broiler.
6. Remove the salmon from the broiler and bake it for an additional 6-7 minutes at 425°F.
7. Take the dish out of the oven, and then start serving it.

Nutritional Info: Calories 267; Fat 8.3g; Sodium 257mg; Carbs 6.4g; Fiber 1.2g; Sugar 2.5g; Protein 40.5g

Enticing Grilled Tomatoes and Shrimp

Preparation time: 5 minutes
Cooking time: 5 minutes
Serves: 2

Ingredients
- 2 cloves garlic, diced or minced, optional.
- 4 tbsps olive oil
- 1 tomato, chopped, medium-sized
- 1 tbsp vinegar, made from red wine
- 2 tbsps fresh basil, chopped
- the black pepper and the salt (to taste)
- 1 pound raw shrimp, peeled.

Instructions:
1. Combine the garlic, olive oil, tomato, vinegar, basil, salt, and pepper in a blender. Blend until completely smooth. Blend until there are no lumps.
2. After putting the shrimp in a bowl, add the mixture on top of them.
3. Place the bowl in the coldest part of the refrigerator for a full hour.
4. Preheat the grill to medium before lighting the charcoal.
5. Skewer the shrimp and cook until they are thoroughly cooked.
6. Spray the grill with Pam cooking spray, add the shrimp, and cook them for two minutes on each side.
7. Indulge in this delectable main dish and the side dish of your choice, then enjoy the meal.

Nutritional Info: Calories 492; Fat 30.3g; Sodium 1979mg; Carbs 5.7g; Fiber 1.2g; Sugar 2.8g; Protein 47.6g

Grilled Chicken Skewers

Preparation time: 10 minutes
Cooking time: 10 minutes
Serves: 4

Ingredients
- 1 ¼ pounds skinless, boneless chicken breast halves
- ¾ cup Pace® Picante Sauce
- 1 tbsp vegetable oil
- 1 tbsp lime juice
- 1 garlic clove, minced or ¼ teaspoon garlic powder
- ½ teaspoon ground cumin

Instructions:
1. Use two layers of plastic wrap to wrap the chicken. Pluck the chicken and pound it with a rolling pin or a meat mallet to a thickness of 12 inches. When preparing the chicken, add salt and pepper to taste. Slice into 1-inch-long strips.
2. In a small bowl, combine the Picante sauce, oil, lime juice, cumin, garlic powder, and salt. Add the chicken and coat.
3. Thread the chicken onto 8 skewers in an accordion fashion. Lightly oil the grill rack and preheat it to medium heat. Cook the chicken on the grill for 10 minutes, turning it over frequently and basting with the Picante sauce mixture. Any remaining Picante sauce mixture must be thrown away.

Nutritional Info: Calories 215; Fat 7g; Sodium 395mg; Carbs 3.7g; Fiber 1.5g; Sugar 3g; Protein 32g

Asian Chicken and Rice Dish

Preparation time: 15 minutes
Cooking time: 35 minutes
Serves: 6

Ingredients
- 2–3 tbsps olive oil
- 1 onion, chopped
- 4 cloves garlic, chopped
- 1 pound chicken thighs, boneless and skinless, cut into bite-size pieces
- 1 whole red bell pepper or 1 cup tomatoes (drained, seeded, chopped)
- 1 cup uncooked long-grain rice (Jasmine recommended)
- 2 cups chicken broth
- 1 cup coconut milk, from canned (shake well before use)
- 2 tbsps regular soy sauce
- 2 tsp Asian fish sauce
- 1–2 tsp chili powder, depending on desired heat
- ¼ cup freshly chopped Thai basil
- Garnishes: lime wedges, roasted chopped peanuts

Instructions:
1. In a sizable nonstick skillet, heat the oil over medium-high heat. In a skillet, cook the onion until it is soft. For one more minute, stir in the garlic. If more oil is required, add it. Stir in the chicken for 2-3 minutes, or until just barely browned.
2. In a sizable mixing bowl, combine the bell peppers or tomatoes, rice, broth, coconut milk, soy sauce, fish sauce, and chili powder. Bring it to a boil, then immediately lower the heat to a simmer. For a further 20 minutes, or until the rice is soft and the liquid has been absorbed, simmer the rice, covered, on the stovetop.
3. Remove from the heat and set aside for 10 minutes, covered. Serve immediately with lime wedges and peanuts after gently tossing with Thai basil.

Nutritional Info: Calories 566; Fat 33.3g; Sodium 664mg; Carbs 31.5g; Fiber 2g; Sugar 3g; Protein 34.8g

Shrimp-Stuffed Tomatoes with Spinach

Preparation time: 10 minutes
Cooking time: None
Serves: 3

Ingredients
- ⅔ pound shrimp, cooked
- 3 tbsps plain, fat-free Greek yogurt.
- 1 teaspoon dried dill
- 3 medium tomatoes
- the black pepper and the salt (to taste)
- 1 cup spinach, roughly chopped

Instructions:
1. Blend the spinach, shrimp, yogurt, spices, and other ingredients in a blender until smooth.
2.
2. Remove the tomato's center pulp with a spoon.
3. Fill the tomatoes with the shrimp mixture and, if you'd like, season them with salt before serving.

Nutritional Info: Calories 136; Fat 1.2g; Sodium 134mg; Carbs 6.5g; Fiber 1.8g; Sugar 4g; Protein 26g

Balsamic Chicken Breast

Preparation time: 10 minutes plus 12 hours for marinating
Cooking time: 10 minutes
Serves: 5

Ingredients
- 5 medium-sized chicken breast halves, skinless and boneless, without the skin, about 1 pound in total
- ¼ cup balsamic vinegar
- 2 fresh garlic cloves, crushed
- 14 tsp black pepper, ground
- 12 medium lemon, peeled and chopped into cubes
- 3 tsp Dijon mustard

Instructions:
1. Place all the ingredients in a blender, excluding the chicken breasts.
2. Combine the ingredients with the chicken, cover, and refrigerate for at least 12 hours to marinate.
3. After taking the chicken out of the marinade, set it aside.
4. Place the chicken breasts on the grill and cook for 5 minutes on each side over high direct heat.
5. Place on a serving tray and top with your favorite vegetables or carbohydrates.

Nutritional Info: Calories 212; Fat 9g; Sodium 96mg; Carbs 14.8g; Fiber 2g; Sugar 4.9g; Protein 20g

Slow Cooked Mediterranean Pork

Preparation time: 20 hours and 10 minutes
Cooking time: 8 hours
Servings: 6

Ingredients
- 5 pounds pork shoulder - boneless
- ¼ cup olive oil
- 2 tsps oregano, dried
- ¼ cup lemon juice
- 2 tsps mustard
- 2 tsps mint, chopped
- 3 garlic cloves, minced
- 2 tsps pesto sauce
- Salt and black pepper to taste

Instructions:
1. In a bowl, combine the olive oil, lemon juice, oregano, mint, mustard, garlic, pecorino, salt, and pepper. To combine, whisk everything together.
2. Marinate the pork for two hours, then cover and chill for ten hours. Flip the pork shoulder and leave it outside for a further 10 hours.
3. Transfer the ingredients and the prepared juices to your slow cooker. 4. Cook on low for 8 hours, covered. Find, slice, divide between plates, and serve.

Nutritional Info: Calories 320 kcal; Fat: 31 g; Carbs: 21 g; Protein: 23g

Fried Mahi Mahi Bites

Preparation time: 10 minutes
Cooking time: 15 minutes
Serves: 4

Ingredients
- 3 mahi mahi fillets (roughly 6–7 ounces each)
- ½ cup tapioca flour
- ⅓ cup almond flour
- 1 tablespoon onion powder
- 1 ½ teaspoons salt
- 2 eggs
- 3 tablespoons coconut oil
- 1 lime

Instructions:
1. Using a kitchen knife, cut the mahi mahi fillets into 1.5″ x 1.5″ cubes. Place aside.
2. In a sizable basin or container, combine the tapioca flour, almond flour, onion powder, and salt.
3. Beat the eggs in a different basin or container.
4. Add the coconut oil to a large skillet that has been heated to medium-high.
5. Working in batches, add the mahi bites to the whisked eggs, then add them to the flour mixture. Shake the bowl or container to thoroughly coat the fish.
6. Drop the fish into the hot coconut oil and cook for 1 minute before flipping the pieces with kitchen tongs and continuing to fry for an additional 45 to 1 minute. After that, flip the fish pieces on their unfried sides for about 30 seconds, or just long enough for all the sides to turn golden. To avoid overfilling the pan, you might need to work in batches.
7. Before serving, cut the lime in half and spritz it with lime juice.

Nutritional Info: Calories 921; Fat 50g; Sodium 934mg; Carbs 88.9g; Fiber 44g; Sugar 3g; Protein 30g

Salmon With Salsa

Preparation time: 15 minutes
Cooking time: 8 minutes
Servings: 2

Ingredients
For Salsa:
- 1 cup fresh pineapple, chopped
- ½ cup bell pepper (red), seeded and chopped
- 2 tbsp. onion, chopped
- 1 tbsp. fresh lemon juice
- Pinch Black pepper, ground, as required

For Salmon:
- (5-oz.) (1-inch thick) salmon fillets
- Pinch salt
- Pinch Black pepper, ground, as required
- 1 tbsp. extra-virgin olive oil
- 1 tbsp. fresh cilantro leaves, chopped

Instructions:
1. To make the salad, combine the other ingredients in a dish with the pineapple.
2. Refrigerate until ready to serve.
3. Season the salmon with salt and black pepper and sauté it.
4. Heat the oil in a large pan over a medium heat.
5. Add the salmon and cook for about 4 minutes, with the skins facing up.
6. Carefully flip the fillets over, then cook for an additional 4 minutes.
7. Divide the salt between the two plates and add the salmon fillets.

Nutritional Info: Calories: 304 kcal; Fat: 16 g; Carbs: 14.2 g; Protein: 28.4 g

Balsamic Grilled Basa

Preparation time: 8 minutes
Cooking time: 10 minutes
Serves: 4

Ingredients
- 4 3.5-ounce basa fillets
- 1 teaspoon fresh rosemary, chopped
- the black pepper and the salt (to taste)
- ½ cup balsamic vinegar
- 1 tbsp extra-virgin olive oil
- 4 tbsps lemon juice, freshly squeezed
- 4 ½ cups baby spinach

Instructions:
1. In a mixing bowl, whisk together the vinegar, lemon juice, and olive oil.
2. After drizzling the salmon with the marinade, place it in the fridge for about 45 minutes so it can soak up the flavors.
3. Take the fish out of the refrigerator and season it with the herbs and spices.
4. Lay the fillets out on the grill in a single layer and grill them for about 5 minutes on each side, or until the fish starts to flake.
5. Position the plate so that it is resting on a bed of baby spinach.

Nutritional Info: Calories 232; Fat 13g; Sodium 99mg; Carbs 7.7g; Fiber 0.8g; Sugar 5.3g; Protein 19.5g

Italian Instant Pot Fish

Preparation time: 10 minutes
Cooking time: 15 minutes
Serves: 4

Ingredients
- ¼ cup water
- 4 frozen white fish fillets, about 3-4 ounce each
- 12 cherry tomatoes
- 12-14 black olives
- 2 tablespoons marinated baby capers
- ⅓ cup sliced roasted red peppers
- 2 tablespoons olive oil
- ½ teaspoon salt
- A pinch of chili flakes
- Garnish: chopped fresh parsley or basil (optional)

Instructions:
1. Add water to the Instant Pot.
2. Add frozen fish fillets to the water. The other ingredients should be added (spread them out around and on top). Sprinkle with sea salt and chili flakes and drizzle with olive oil.
3. Shut the lid. 4. Set to "Manual" or "Pressure" Cook for four minutes under high pressure. The Instant Pot will begin to generate pressure and begin cooking after three beeps. Allow the pressure to release naturally for 7 to 8 minutes after the timer sounds before doing the quick release to allow the steam out.
4. Open the cover and carefully remove the fish fillets using a spatula. Place the cooked items on top of the soup, then serve. Add a little chopped parsley or basil as a garnish.

Nutritional Info: Calories 1099; Fat 76g; Sodium 2922mg; Carbs 15g; Fiber 6g; Sugar 8.5g; Protein 87.5g

Balearic Beef Brisket Bowl

Preparation time: 0 minutes
Cooking time: 50 minutes
Servings: 2

Ingredients
- ½-cup manto negro dry red wine (Spanish or Mallorca dry red wine)
- ⅓-cup olives, pitted and chopped
- 14.5-oz tomatoes with juice (diced)
- 5-cloves garlic, chopped
- ½-tsp dried rosemary
- Salt and pepper
- 2 ½ lbs. Beef brisket
- Olive oil
- 1-tbsp fresh parsley, finely chopped
- 1 ½-cups sautéed green beans

Instructions:
1. Add the tomatoes, garlic, and rosemary to your slow cooker after adding the dry wine and olives.
2. Sprinkle salt and pepper over the beef brisket. Put the seasoned meat on top of the wine-tomato mixture. Leap about half of the mixture over the mixture. For six hours on high heat, cover the slow cooker and simmer the food until it is fork-tender.
3. Move the cooked bacon to a cutting board. For ten minutes, wrap the meat in foil and let it stand.
4. Add a drizzle of olive oil. Slice the brisket into six equal pieces against the grain, transfer to a serving platter, and then spread some sauce over the meat slices. Add a sprinkle of parsley.
5. Plate the green beans with the remaining sauce.

Nutritional Info: Calories: 370 kcal; Fat: 18 g; Carbs: 6 g; Protein: 41g

Especial Glazed Salmon

Preparation time: 45 minutes
Cooking time: 10 minutes
Servings: 4

Ingredients
- 4 pieces salmon fillets, 5 oz. each
- 1 tbsp. coconut aminos
- 2 tsp. olive oil
- 1 tsp. ginger, minced
- 1 tsp. garlic, minced
- 2 tbsp. sugar-free ketchup
- 2 tbsp. dry white wine
- 2 tbsp. red boat fish sauce, low-sodium

Instructions:
1. Combine the coconut aminos, garlic, ginger, and fish sauce in a bowl. Mix.
2. Stir in the salmon and set aside for 15 to 20 minutes.
3. Place a skillet or pan over medium heat.
4. Pour in the oil and heat it up.
5. Add the salmon filets and cook for 3 to 4 minutes on each side over high heat.
6. Remove the dish when it is crispy.
7. Add the wine and salt.
8. Simmer for 5 minutes on low heat.
9. Return the salmon to the glass and flip it until both sides are coated with glass. 10.
10. Serve and enjoy yourself!

Nutritional Info: Calories: 372 kcal; Fat: 24 g; Carbs: 3 g; Protein: 35 g

Healthy Vegetable Fried Rice

Preparation time: 15 minutes
Cooking time: 10 minutes
Servings: 4

Ingredients:
For the Sauce:
- ⅓ cup garlic vinegar
- 1 ½ tbsp dark molasses
- 1 tsp onion powder

For the Fried Rice:
- 1 tsp olive oil
- 2 lightly beaten whole eggs + 4 egg whites
- 1 cup of frozen mixed vegetables
- 1 cup frozen edamame
- 2 cups cooked brown rice

Instructions:
1. To prepare the sauce, combine the garlic wine, butter, and onion powder in a glass jar. Shuffle well.
2. In a large wok or skillet, heat the oil over medium heat. Add the eggs and the egg whites and simmer for about a minute, or until the eggs are set.
3. Use a spatula or spoon to break eggs into small pieces. Add frozen blended vegetables and frozen edamame. Cook for 4 minutes while frequently stirring.
4. Add the brown rice and sauce to the mixture of vegetables and eggs.5. Cook for five.
5 minutes, or until thoroughly heated Serve immediately.

Nutritional Info: Calories: 210 kcal; Fat: 6 g; Carbs: 28 g; Protein: 13 g

Chicken Meatloaf

Preparation time: 15 minutes
Cooking time: 45 minutes
Serves: 8

Ingredients
- 5 ½ pounds lean ground chicken
- 1 medium onion
- 1 green pepper
- 12 cups zucchini
- 12 cups broccoli
- 2 stalks celery
- 1 ounce chopped up mushrooms
- 1 teaspoon thyme
- ¼ cup fresh basil
- ¼ cup fresh parsley
- salt and pepper, to taste
- 4 egg whites.
- 2 cups rolled organic oats in the organic form
- 1 bulb garlic, minced

Instructions:
1. Spray a skillet with Pam cooking spray before adding the onions, peppers, zucchini, broccoli, celery, and mushrooms. Cook the vegetables for a few minutes over medium heat.
2. Add the garlic.1 to 2 minutes prior to the vegetables' being finished cooking, turn off the heat, and then let the vegetables cool for about 5 minutes.
3. Add the cooked vegetables and the remaining ingredients to a big bowl and stir everything together.
4. Before putting the batter in the oven, place it in loaf pans or any other baking dish that has been greased with Pam.
5. Bake for 40 minutes at 425°F in an oven preheated to that temperature.
6. After taking the meatloaf out of the oven, allow it to cool for 45 minutes before serving.
7. Eat the chicken after cutting it into 8 equal pieces.

Nutritional Info: Calories 600; Fat 27.8g; Sodium 395mg; Carbs 26g; Fiber 6g; Sugar 8g; Protein 64g

Tahini Chicken Shawarma

Preparation time: 4 minutes
Cooking time: 4 minutes
Serves: 3

Ingredients
- 1 cup cucumbers, shredded
- ¼ cup nonfat Greek yogurt, either the strained or the plain variety
- 1 tbsp tahini
- 2 tbsps lemon juice
- ½ teaspoon salt, divided
- 1 tbsp and 1 level teaspoon garlic powder
- 1 teaspoon, weighed and level, curry powder
- freshly ground black pepper, to taste
- 1 pound chicken breasts, boneless and skinless without excess fat or gristle
- 1 tbsp coconut oil
- large romaine lettuce leaves

Instructions:
1. Increase the grill's heat setting to medium.
2. In a medium bowl, combine the diced cucumber, yogurt, tahini, lemon juice, and ¼ teaspoon salt. Place aside.
3. Add the remaining ¼ teaspoon of salt, the pepper, the curry powder, and the garlic powder to a second medium bowl. The chicken breasts should be cut lengthwise into quarter-inch-wide strips before being added to the spice mixture to coat them. Combine the ingredients with 1 tbsp of oil by tossing them together.
4. Place the chicken on the grill and cook it, turning it once, for about 2 minutes on each side. Do this repeatedly until the chicken is cooked through.
5. To plate the dish, start by smearing a sizable lettuce leaf with a quarter cup of the cucumber-yogurt sauce. After that, scatter a fourth of the chicken over the sauce. Eat it by rolling it up like a taco!

Nutritional Info: Calories 404; Fat 15g; Sodium 723mg; Carbs 10.6g; Fiber 2.4g; Sugar 2.6g; Protein 56g

Vegetarian Kebabs

Preparation time: 15 minutes
Cooking time: 6 minutes
Servings: 4

Ingredients
- 2 tbsps balsamic vinegar
- 1 tbsp olive oil
- 1 tsp dried parsley
- 2 tbsps water
- 2 sweet peppers
- 2 red onions, peeled
- 2 zucchinis, trimmed

Instructions:
1. Cut the sweet peppers and onions into medium-sized squares.2. After that, shave the zucchini. Place each vegetable on a skewer. Next, add olive oil, dried parsley, water, and balsamic vinegar to the shallow bowl.
2. Brush the vegetables with the olive oil mixture and place them on a preheated grill set to 390 degrees Fahrenheit. Cooking time for the kebabs should be three minutes each side, or until the vegetables are golden brown.

Nutritional Info: Calories: 88 kcal; Fat 3.9g; Carbs 13 g; Protein 2.4 g

Pork With Couscous

Preparation time: 10 minutes
Cooking time: 7 hours
Servings: 6

Ingredients
- ½ pounds pork loin boneless and trimmed
- ¾ cup chicken stock
- 4 tbsps olive oil
- ½ tbsp sweet paprika
- 1 and ¼ tsp sage, dried
- ½ tbsp garlic powder
- ¼ tsp rosemary, dried
- ¼ tsp marjoram, dried
- 1 tsp basil, dried
- 1 tsp oregano, dried
- Salt and black pepper to taste
- cups couscous, cooked

Instructions:
1. In a bowl, whisk together the oil, stock, paprika, garlic powder, rosemary, thyme, marjoram, oregano, salt, and pepper. Place a pork loin in your slow cooker.
2. Stir in the spice mixture and stock, cover, and cook on low for seven hours. Slice the pork, then add it back to the saucepan with the cooking juices. Separate the plates, then serve with couscous on the side.

Nutritional Info: Calories: 320 kcal; Fat: 31 g; Carbs: 21 g; Protein: 23g

Spanish Mussels

Preparation time: 10 minutes
Cooking time: 23 minutes
Servings: 4

Ingredients
- 1 tbsp. olive oil
- 1 lb. mussels, scrubbed
- Pinch Pepper to taste
- 1 cups tomatoes, canned and crushed
- 1 shallot, chopped
- 2 garlic cloves, minced
- 2 cups low-sodium vegetable stock
- ⅓ cup cilantro, chopped

Instructions:
1. Heat the shallot in a pan over medium heat for three minutes, stirring constantly.
2. Stir in the garlic, stock, tomatoes, and pepper, then reduce to a low heat and cook for 10 minutes.
3. Add the mussels and the cilantro, then mix.
4. Cover and cook for a further 10 minutes.
5. Serve and enjoy yourself!

Nutritional Info: Calories: 210 kcal; Fat: 2 g; Carbs: 5 g; Protein: 8 g

Cauliflower Mashed Potatoes

Preparation time: 10 minutes
Cooking time: 10 minutes
Servings: 4

Ingredients:
- 16 cups water (enough to cover cauliflower)
- 1 head cauliflower (about 3 pounds), trimmed and cut into florets
- 4 garlic cloves
- 1 tbsp olive oil
- ¼ tsp salt
- ⅛ tsp freshly ground black pepper
- 2 tsps dried parsley

Instructions:
1. Bring a large saucepan of water to a boil, then add the cauliflower and garlic.
2. Ten minutes to cook, then strain. Move it back to the heated pan and let it sit there with the lid on for two to three minutes.
3. In a food processor, combine the cauliflower and garlic. To make it smooth, add the olive oil, salt, pepper, and puree. Taste and correct the salt and pepper.
4. Remove from the heat, add the powder, and stir until combined. If desired, add more olive oil as a garnish. Serve immediately.

Nutritional Info: Calories: 87 kcal; Fat: 4 g; Carbs: 12 g; Protein: 4 g

Avocado Tuna Cucumber Roll

Preparation time: 8 minutes
Cooking time: None
Serves: 1

Ingredients
- ¼ cucumber
- 1 can tuna
- ½ avocado
- 2 tsp mustard in the yellow color (yellow or Dijon)
- salt and pepper (to taste)

Instructions:
1. In a mixing bowl, combine the tuna, avocado, and mustard.
2. Slice the cucumber into pieces that are one-fiftyth of an inch thick.
3. Before discarding the cucumber slices, take the slices and remove the seeds (either cut them out with a knife or push them out with your fingers).
4. Make sure to completely fill the center of the cucumbers with the tuna mixture.
5. Season with salt and pepper to taste and enjoy!

Nutritional Info: Calories 334; Fat 17g; Sodium 700mg; Carbs 14.7g; Fiber 8g; Sugar 4.6g; Protein 35g

Balsamic Salmon Steaks

Preparation time: 10 minutes plus 4 to 6 hours for marinating
Cooking time: 20 minutes
Serves: 3

Ingredients
- 6 5-ounce salmon or tilapia fillets, cut into fillets.
- 4 tbsps diluted fermented soy sauce
- 4 tbsps balsamic vinegar
- 4 tbsps thinly sliced green onions
- 4 stevia packets in total
- 4 whole garlic cloves, minced
- 1 ½ tsp ginger powder
- ½ pinch dried crushed red pepper flakes
- 1 teaspoon sesame oil
- ½ teaspoon salt

Instructions:
1. Arrange the salmon fillets in a non-permeable glass dish that is about the middle size.
2. Combine the toasted sesame oil, soy sauce, vinegar, green onions, garlic, ginger, and crushed red pepper flakes in another dish of the same size. 3. Garnish with more green onions if desired.
3. Whisk all of the ingredients together before pouring them over the fish. Make sure to cover and keep the salmon cool while marinating it for 4 to 6 hours in the fridge.
4. To prepare an outside grill, move the coals to a spot about 5 inches away from the grate. Next, drizzle a thin layer of oil over the grate.
5. Position the fillets on a grill five inches from the embers and cook them for 10 minutes per inch of thickness, measured at the thickest section of the fillet, or until the fish easily breaks apart when tested with a fork. You should turn the meat over halfway through the cooking process.

Nutritional Info: Calories 544; Fat 26g; Sodium 1944mg; Carbs 12.8g; Fiber 0.8g; Sugar 9g; Protein 60.6g

Broccoli With Garlic And Lemon

Preparation time: 2 minutes
Cooking time: 4 minutes
Servings: 4

Ingredients
- 1 cup water
- 4 cups broccoli florets
- 1 tsp olive oil
- 1 tbsp minced garlic
- 1 tsp lemon zest
- Pinch Salt
- 1 tsp freshly ground black pepper

Instructions:
1. In a small saucepan of water, boil the broccoli for two to three minutes. The broccoli should maintain its vibrant green hue. Rinse the water off the broccoli.
2. In a small sauté pan over medium heat, heat the oil.
3. Cook for 30 seconds after adding the garlic.
4. Add the broccoli, lemon zest, salt, pepper, and lemon juice. Well combined and served.

Nutritional Info: Calories: 38 kcal; Fat: 1 g; Carbs: 5 g; Protein: 3 g

Salmon And Veggie Parcel

Preparation time: 15 minutes
Cooking time: 20 minutes
Servings: 6

Ingredients
- (3-oz.) salmon fillets
- Pinch salt
- 1 tsp Black pepper, ground as required
- 2 bell peppers (yellow and red), seeded and cubed
- 2 tomatoes, cubed
- 1 small onion, sliced thinly
- ½ cup fresh parsley, chopped
- ¼ cup extra-virgin olive oil
- 1 tbsp. fresh lemon juice

Instructions:
1. Preheat the oven to 400°F.
2. Arrange six pieces of foil on a flat surface.
3. Season 1 salmon fillet per piece of foil with salt and black pepper.
4. In a mixing bowl, combine the bell peppers, tomato, and onion.
5. Spread the vegetable mixture evenly over each fillet and top with parsley and capers.
6. Drizzle with oil and lemon juice.
7. To seal the salmon mixture, fold the foil over it.
8. Arrange the foil packets on a large baking sheet in a single layer.
9. Bake for approximately 20 minutes.
10. Provide hot food.

Nutritional Info: Calories: 224 kcal; Fat: 14 g; Carbs: 8.7 g; Protein: 18.2 g

Garlic Shrimp Etouffee

Preparation time: 15 minutes
Cooking time: 25 minutes
Serves: 4

Ingredients
- 3 tbsps lard
- 1 small sweet onion diced
- 1 stalk celery diced
- ½ bell pepper diced (AIP: sub 1 more stalk celery or 1 small carrot)
- ¼ cup cassava flour
- 2 large cloves garlic pressed
- 1 tbsp Cajun seasoning or ½ teaspoon garlic powder, ½ teaspoon onion powder, ¼ teaspoon Italian seasoning, 1 teaspoon ginger powder, 1 teaspoon horseradish powder, and ¼ teaspoon Himalayan salt
- 1 tbsp dried parsley
- ½ teaspoon Himalayan salt
- 1 to 2 tsp Frank's Red Hot or lemon juice
- 1 pound medium shrimp peeled, deveined, tails removed and strained very well
- 3 cups bone broth, fish, chicken or pork
- 1 bay leaf
- lemon wedges

Instructions:
1. Pristine Saute. Add the fat, onion, celery, and bell pepper when the dish starts to smell hot. Mix well.
2. Cook, stirring occasionally, for 7 minutes, or until browned and slightly caramelized.
3. Press "CANCEL" before vigorously stirring in the cassava flour to bring the mixture together. adding garlic
4. Cajun seasoning, parsley, salt, and hot sauce
5. PRÉS AUTÉ. Once LESS is lit up, press ADJUST.
6. Add 1 cup of the bone broth while stirring constantly to avoid lumps. Once the mixture is smooth, add the bay leaf and gradually stir in the remaining 2 cups of broth.
7. To avoid sticking, simmer while stirring and scraping the bottom every few minutes. Cook in this manner for 10 to 15 minutes, or until the sauce has thickened and been reduced to ⅔.
8. Stir in the shrimp. Cook for two minutes while stirring constantly. Click CANCEL.
9. (Shrimp will continue to cook slightly in the hot gravy; thus, it is best to turn off the heat underneath just before they appear to be finished.)
10. Dish it up in dishes with a splash of spicy sauce and lemon wedges.

Nutritional Info: Calories 253; Fat 10.8g; Sodium 1290mg; Carbs 14.6g; Fiber 1.6g; Sugar 5.4g; Protein 25g

Mahi Mahi Taco

Preparation time: 4 minutes
Cooking time: 15 minutes
Serves: 2

Ingredients
- 4 cups shredded cabbage
- 2 filets mahi mahi, about 4 ounces each
- 2 cups riced cauliflower
- 1 tbsp taco seasoning
- ½ cup mango salsa
- ½ tablespoon plus 1 teaspoon avocado oil
- 1 tablespoon lime juice
- ¼ cup cilantro, roughly chopped
- 2 tablespoons spicy chipotle mayo
- ½ large avocado
- ½ cup red onion, thinly sliced
- ½ cup apple cider vinegar
- water
- 1 teaspoon salt
- optional toppings: jalapeños, cilantro, lime wedges

Instructions:
1. Coat a medium-sized saucepan with Pam cooking spray and heat it over a medium-high flame.
2. Add the onions and peppers when the oil has entirely been absorbed, and continue to cook the mixture until the onions are transparent.
3. Before serving, thoroughly combine the remaining ingredients, excluding the canned tomatoes and lettuce.
4. Combine the ingredients in a pot and bring the mixture to a boil. Once the chicken or turkey has been ground, continue with this step.
5. Turn off the heat and pour off any liquid that has accumulated in the pan.
6. Re-heat it on the burner, this time with the heat set to a temperature that lies halfway between medium and low, and then stir in the canned tomatoes.
7. After you've finished cooking, continue for an additional 5 minutes. Serve it to the visitors after taking it off the heat.
8. There are two ways to prepare this dish: either slice the romaine lettuce and serve it as a salad with the chicken mixture on top, or use the individual romaine leaves as taco shells and fill each one with the chicken mixture.

Nutritional Info: Calories 685; Fat 76g; Sodium 2113mg; Carbs 36g; Fiber 11.6g; Sugar 14.4g; Protein 76g

Oregano Chicken Tacos Salad

Preparation time: 10 minutes
Cooking time: 15 to 20 minutes
Serves: 3

Ingredients
- ⅔ pound chicken or turkey ground meat
- 1 yellow onion, cut into 12 large slices
- dried red pepper, chopped
- 1 level teaspoon dried oregano
- 2 tsp chili pepper
- ½ teaspoon black pepper
- 1 packet stevia
- 1 small can chopped tomatoes, drained
- Salt to taste
- 6 romaine lettuce leaves

Instructions:
1. Coat a medium-sized saucepan with Pam cooking spray and heat it over a medium-high flame.
2. Add the onions and peppers when the oil has entirely been absorbed, and continue to cook the mixture until the onions are transparent.
3. Before serving, thoroughly combine the remaining ingredients, excluding the canned tomatoes and lettuce.
4. Combine the ingredients in a pot and bring the mixture to a boil. Once the chicken or turkey has been ground, continue with this step.
5. Turn off the heat and pour off any liquid that has accumulated in the pan.
6. Re-heat it on the burner, this time with the heat set to a temperature that lies halfway between medium and low, and then stir in the canned tomatoes.
7. After you've finished cooking, continue for an additional 5 minutes. Serve it to the visitors after taking it off the heat.
8. There are two ways to prepare this dish: either slice the romaine lettuce and serve it as a salad with the chicken mixture on top, or use the individual romaine leaves as taco shells and fill each one with the chicken mixture.

Nutritional Info: Calories 343; Fat 12g; Sodium 1170mg; Carbs 32g; Fiber 7g; Sugar 11.7g; Protein 32g

Mackerel And Orange Medley

Preparation time: 10 minutes
Cooking time: 10 minutes
Servings: 4

Ingredients
- 4 mackerel fillets, skinless and boneless
- 1 spring onion, chopped
- 1 tsp. olive oil
- 1-inch ginger piece, grated
- Pinch Black pepper, as needed
- Juice and zest of 1 whole orange
- 1 cup low-sodium fish stock

Instructions:
1. Rub olive oil on the fillets after seasoning them with black pepper.
2. Place the stock, orange juice, ginger, orange zest, and onion in the Instant Pot.
3. Set a skillet on the table and add the fillets.
4. Close the lid and cook on HIGH pressure for 10 minutes.
5. Let the pressure drop naturally over a ten-minute period.
6. Arrange the fillets on plates and drizzle the orange sauce from the saucepan over the fish.
7. Enjoy!

Nutritional Info: Calories: 200 kcal; Fat: 4 g; Carbs: 19 g; Protein: 14 g

Mediterranean Lamb Chops

Preparation time: 10 minutes
Cooking time: 10 minutes
Servings: 2

Ingredients
- lamb shoulder chops, 8 ounces each
- 2 tbsps Dijon mustard
- 2 tbsps Balsamic vinegar
- 1 tbsp garlic, chopped
- ½ cup olive oil
- 1 tbsp shredded fresh basil

Instructions:
1. Lay the lamb chops out on a shallow baking tray after patting them dry with a kitchen towel.
2. Take a bowl, add the Dijon mustard, balsamic vinegar, garlic, and pepper, and stir to combine.
3. Once the mixture is smooth, very gently whisk in the oil until it is incorporated.
4. Add the basil.
5. Pour the marinade over the lamb chops, then toss to thoroughly coat both sides.
6. Cover the chops and let them marinate for 1–4 hours (in the refrigerator).
7. Take the chops out and let them sit for 30 minutes to let the temperature reach its usual level.
8. Heat up your grill to a medium temperature and add oil to the grates.
9. The lamb chops should be cooked for 5 to 10 minutes on each side, or until both sides are browned.
10. The chops are ready when the center registers 145 degrees Fahrenheit. Serve and have fun!

Nutritional Info: Calories: 521 kcal; Fat: 45 g; Carbs: 3.5 g; Protein: 22g

Lemongrass Shrimp/Chicken Soup

Preparation time: 15 minutes
Cooking time: 20 minutes
Serves: 4

Ingredients
- 6 cups stock, preferably organic chicken, beef, or vegetable
- 2 tsp lemongrass, frozen
- 3-4 lime leaves
- 3 to 4 cloves garlic, minced
- 1 slice of ginger around the size of the index finger
- 3 tbsps fish sauce or 4 tsp soy sauce (use wheat-free soy sauce for gluten-free diets)
- 1 tbsp lime juice, freshly squeezed
- 1 fresh red chili pepper or half a teaspoon of dried chili powder
- Vegetables (mushrooms, cauliflower, bok choy, broccoli), as you like
- 30 shrimp or 3 chicken breasts, cooked
- ½ can coconut milk
- 12 cups of fresh basil/cilantro

Instructions:
1. The first four ingredients should be heated to a boil after being combined.
2. Reduce the heat to a level between low and medium and add the other ingredients, excluding the final three.
3. Simmer for around 15 minutes (until the vegetables are cooked to your liking).
4. Thoroughly combine the meat with a small amount of coconut milk.
5. Continue to cook the dish for an additional three to five minutes (until it lightly bubbles again).
6. Before setting the bowls on the table, add a finishing touch by sprinkling chopped cilantro or basil over the top of each bowl's share.

Nutritional Info: Calories 597; Fat 35.8g; Sodium 887mg; Carbs 12g; Fiber 2.8g; Sugar 4.8g; Protein 58g

Brown Rice Pilaf

Preparation time: 5 minutes
Cooking time: 10 minutes
Servings: 4

Ingredients
- 1 cup low-sodium vegetable broth
- ½ tbsp olive oil
- 1 garlic clove, minced
- 1 scallion, thinly sliced
- 1 tbsp minced onion flakes
- 1 cup instant brown rice
- ⅛ tsp freshly ground black pepper

Instructions:
1. In a sauce pan, combine the vegetable broth, olive oil, garlic, scallions, and minced onion flakes. Bring it to a boil.
2. Add the rice and boil it again. After 10 minutes, adjust the heat and simmer.
3. Remove and set aside for 5 minutes.
4. Use a fork to fluff, then season with black pepper.

Nutritional Info: Calories: 100 kcal; Fat: 2 g; Carbs: 19 g; Protein: 2 g

Lemony Shrimp with Cocktail Sauce

Preparation time: 10 minutes
Cooking time: 5 minutes
Serves: 8

Ingredients
- 2 cups water
- 1 tbsp sea salt
- 2 pounds large or jumbo shrimp deveined, fresh or frozen
- 2 lemons
- Ice bath

Cocktail sauce:
- ¾ cup sugar-free ketchup
- 1 ½ tbsps horseradish
- 1 tbsp apple cider vinegar
- 1 teaspoon lemon juice
- 1 teaspoon coconut aminos
- ½ teaspoon hot sauce

Instructions:
1. Prepare the coffee sauce by whisking all of the ingredients together.
2. While you cook the shrimp, refrigerate it.
3. Add water and sea salt to the Instant Pot.
4. Cut the lemons in half, squeeze the juice into the pot, and then add the lemon halves.
5. Add the shrimp and combine them.
6. Secure the Instant Pot and switch the steam release knob to "Sealing."
7. If the shrimp has defrosted, cook for 30 seconds on high. While the shrimp are cooking, prepare an ice bath. Quick release pressure
8. Microwave frozen shrimp for 1 minute on high. During the cooking of the shrimp, prepare an ice bath. Quick release pressure
9. Transfer the shrimp to the ice bath with a slotted spoon so they can stop cooking.
10. Peel the shrimp.
11. To have something to grip onto while eating, I prefer to leave the tail on.
12. Accompany with a cocktail auce.

Nutritional Info: Calories 126; Fat 0.7g; Sodium 1247mg; Carbs 8g; Fiber 0.6g; Sugar 5.4g; Protein 23g

Snack and Appetizer Recipes

Garlic Salsa

Preparation time: 10 minutes
Cooking time: 2 ½ hours to 3 hours
Serves: 25

Ingredients
- 10 plum tomatoes
- 2 garlic cloves
- 1 small onion, cut into wedges
- 1–2 jalapeño peppers
- ½ cup chopped fresh cilantro
- ½ teaspoon sea salt, optional

Instructions:
1. Take out the tomatoes' cores. Make a little slit in each tomato. A garlic clove should be placed in each slice.
2. Put all of the tomatoes and onions in a 3-quart slow cooker.
3. Cut the jalapenos' stems off. (If you want a milder version, remove the seeds.) The jalapenos should be put in a slow cooker.
4. Covered, cook on high for 2 to 3 hours, or until the vegetables are tender. Some might start to turn brown. Give the lid some time to cool for at least two hours. The tomato mixture, cilantro, and salt, if desired, should all be combined in a blender. Blend until combined and covered.

Nutritional Info: Calories 19; Fat 0g; Sodium 50mg; Carbs 4.9g; Fiber 0.3g; Sugar 4.4g; Protein 0.2g

Curried Almonds with Turmeric

Preparation time: 5 minutes
Cooking time: 3½–4½ hours
Serves: 64

Ingredients
- 2 tbsps coconut oil
- 1 tbsp curry powder
- ½ teaspoon sea salt
- ⅛ teaspoon turmeric
- ⅛ teaspoon paprika
- ⅛ teaspoon onion powder
- ⅛ teaspoon garlic powder
- ⅛ teaspoon sugar
- 1 pound blanched almonds

Instructions:
1. In a mixing dish, combine the spices and coconut oil.
2. Pour the liquid into the slow cooker, then add the almonds. To coat, thoroughly combine all ingredients.
3. Cover. 2 to 3 hours on low heat. Turn up the volume all the way. After revealing the cooker, cook for one to one and a half hours.
4. Serve at room temperature or warm.

Nutritional Info: Calories 45; Fat 4g; Sodium 18mg; Carbs 1.6g; Fiber 1g; Sugar 0.3g; Protein 1.5g

Hoisin Button Mushrooms

Preparation time: 10 minutes
Cooking time: 5 to 6 hours
Serves: 10

Ingredients
- 24 ounces whole button mushrooms, trimmed
- 1 small sweet onion, halved, sliced
- ¼ cup water
- 3 cloves garlic, minced
- 2 tbsps gluten-free soy sauce or Bragg's liquid aminos
- 1 tbsp smooth natural peanut butter
- 1 teaspoon rice wine vinegar
- 1 teaspoon sesame oil
- ¼ teaspoon crushed red pepper

Instructions:
1. Spray nonstick cooking spray on the crock.
2. Add the mushrooms and onions to the crock.
3. In a sizable mixing bowl, combine the water, garlic, soy sauce, peanut butter, rice wine vinegar, sesame oil, and crushed red pepper. Pouring this mixture over the mushrooms and onions is necessary.
4. Covered, cook on low for 5 to 6 hours.
5. Before removing the mushrooms with a slotted spoon for serving, gently fold them into the sauce. The mushrooms are served on toothpicks.
6. Garnish with green onion and sesame seeds, if desired.

Nutritional Info: Calories 228; Fat 1.8g; Sodium 124mg; Carbs 54.9g; Fiber 8.3g; Sugar 3.4g; Protein 7.6g

Mexican Meat Dip

Preparation time: 15 to 20 minutes
Cooking time: 2 to 3 hours
Serves: 15

Ingredients
- 1 pound low-fat ground beef or turkey
- 1 8-ounce package low-fat Mexican cheese, grated
- 1 16-ounce jar mild, thick, and chunky Picante salsa, or thick and chunky salsa
- 1 6-ounce can vegetarian refried beans

Instructions:
1. In a mixing dish, combine the spices and coconut oil.
2. Pour the liquid into the slow cooker, then add the almonds. To coat, thoroughly combine all ingredients.
3. Cover. 2 to 3 hours on low heat. Turn up the volume all the way. After revealing the cooker, cook for one to one and a half hours.
4. Serve at room temperature or warm.

Nutritional Info: Calories 162; Fat 8g; Sodium 638mg; Carbs 10g; Fiber 0.6g; Sugar 0.2g; Protein 12.6g

Veggie and Cheese Dip

Preparation time: 10 minutes
Cooking time: 3 to 4 hours
Serves: 3

Ingredients
- 1 10-ounce bag fresh baby spinach, roughly chopped
- 1 13.75-ounce can quartered artichoke hearts, drained and chopped
- 1 8-ounce brick reduced-fat cream cheese
- 1 cup non-fat plain Greek yogurt
- 1 cup shredded mozzarella cheese
- ½ cup grated Parmesan cheese
- ½ cup chopped onion
- ¼ cup chopped green onion

Instructions:
1. Spray nonstick cooking spray on your crock.
2. In a large crock, combine and thoroughly whisk all of the ingredients.
3. Once the cheese has completely melted and the dip is well cooked, remove the cover and cook on low for 3 to 4 hours.
4. Accompany with fresh carrot sticks, pita bread made without gluten, or brown rice crackers. Garnish with sliced red bell pepper.

Nutritional Info: Calories 164; Fat 6.6g; Sodium 388mg; Carbs 13g; Fiber 5.6g; Sugar 4g; Protein 15g

Almond, Cranberry, and Coconut

Preparation time: 10 minutes
Cooking time: 2 to 3 hours
Serves: 12

Ingredients
- 5 cups gluten-free Cheerios
- 3 cups gluten-free Honey Nut Cheerios
- 1 cup gluten-free oats
- 1 cup dried cranberries
- 2 cups unsweetened shredded coconut
- 2 cups raw almonds, chopped
- ¼ cup melted coconut oil
- ¼ cup honey
- ½ teaspoon cinnamon
- ½ teaspoon salt
- 1 t
- easpoon vanilla

Instructions:
1. Spray nonstick cooking spray on the crock.
2. Evenly distribute Cheerios, Honey Nut Cheerios, gluten-free oats, cranberries, coconut, and almonds throughout the crock.
3. In a mixing bowl, combine the coconut oil, honey, cinnamon, salt, and vanilla. With a rubber spatula, gently toss the cereal in the crock after adding the ingredients to make sure it is all coated.
4. With a paper towel under the lid, cover the pot and cook it for two to three hours on low. Stir the mixture approximately every 45 minutes to prevent it from burning.
5. After the mixture has finished cooking, place it on a baking sheet that has been lined with parchment paper and leave it there to cool for an hour. Serve right away or store it for up to 3 weeks at room temperature in an airtight jar.

Nutritional Info: Calories 252; Fat 10g; Sodium 230mg; Carbs 42.5g; Fiber 3.5g; Sugar 16g; Protein 3.7g

Spicy Prairie Fire Dip

Preparation time: 5 to 10 minutes
Cooking time: 1 to 3 hours
Serves: 10

Ingredients
- 1 cup vegetarian refried fat-free beans (half a 15-oz. can)
- ½ cup shredded fat-free Monterey Jack cheese
- ¼ cup water
- 1 tbsp minced onion
- 1 clove garlic, minced
- 2 tsp chili powder
- hot sauce as desired

Instructions:
1. In a slow cooker, combine all of the ingredients.
2. Cover it with whatever you want. Cook for 1-2 hours on high or low, respectively. Cooked tortilla chips should be used with this dish.
3. Serve with diced avocado and hot sauce as garnish.

Nutritional Info: Calories 34; Fat 0.3g; Sodium 210mg; Carbs 4.4g; Fiber 1.2g; Sugar 1g; Protein 3.5g

Awesome Seven-Layer Dip

Preparation time: 20 minutes
Cooking time: 2 hours
Serves: 10 to 15

Ingredients
- 1 pound lean ground turkey
- 2½ tsp chili powder, divided
- ½ teaspoon kosher salt
- ⅛ teaspoon pepper
- 1 15-ounce can fat-free refried beans
- 1 4-ounce can diced green chilies
- 1 cup non-fat Greek yogurt
- 1 cup salsa
- 1 cup shredded Mexican blend cheese
- 1 2-ounce can sliced black olives
- 2 green onions, sliced

Instructions:
1. In a skillet, brown the ground turkey with a teaspoon of chili powder, salt, and pepper.
2. In the interim, apply nonstick cooking spray on the crock.
3. Layer the refried beans in a layer on the bottom of the crock after mixing them with 1 teaspoon of chili powder.
4. After that, layer the green chilies in dice on top.
5. Evenly distribute the ground turkey over the green chilies.
6. In a mixing dish, combine the Greek yogurt and the remaining ½ teaspoon of chili powder. Pour the mixture over the ground turkey in the crock.
7. Last but not least, add the salsa on top.
8. Place the black olives on top, then put the cheese on top of that.
9. Cook on low for two hours. Top with the green onions just before serving.

Nutritional Info: Calories 139; Fat 6.6g; Sodium 666mg; Carbs 10g; Fiber 4.6g; Sugar 2.2g; Protein 12g

Herbed Pizza Dip

Preparation time: 15 minutes
Cooking time: 5 to 6 hours
Serves: 14

Ingredients
- 1 pound bulk gluten-free turkey sausage
- ⅔ cup chopped onion
- 4 cloves garlic, minced
- 2 15-ounce cans low-sodium tomato sauce
- 1 14.5-ounce can diced tomatoes
- 1 6-ounce can low-sodium tomato paste
- 1 tbsp dried oregano
- 1 tbsp dried basil
- ¾ teaspoon crushed red pepper
- 1½ tsp turbinado sugar
- ½ cup sliced black olives

Instructions:
1. In a big skillet, brown the onion, garlic, and turkey sausage. Take the grease off.
2. In the crock, combine all the remaining ingredients, excluding the olives.
3. Cook on low for 5 to 6 hours, covered. Just before serving, stir in the olives.
4. To make it more nutritious, serve it with a rainbow of bell pepper slices for dipping. Garnish options include minced parsley or microgreens.

Nutritional Info: Calories 149; Fat 9g; Sodium 381mg; Carbs 8.5g; Fiber 2g; Sugar 5g; Protein 8.7g

Gingered Nuts Mix

Preparation time: 15 minutes
Cooking time: 2 hours
Serves: 22

Ingredients
- 1 cup unsalted cashews
- 1 cup unsalted almonds
- 1 cup unsalted pecans
- 1 cup unsalted, shelled pistachios
- ½ cup maple syrup
- ⅓ cup melted coconut oil
- 1 teaspoon ground ginger
- ½ teaspoon sea salt
- ½ teaspoon cinnamon
- ¼ teaspoon ground cloves
- ¼ teaspoon cayenne pepper

Instructions:
1. Spray nonstick cooking spray on the crock.
2. Add the nuts to the crock and stir in the other ingredients, making sure they are all evenly distributed.
3. Before covering the crock, slide a piece of paper towel or a thin dishtowel below the lid. Cook on low heat for an hour, then stir in the nuts. After two hours, stir them once more, then spread them out on a cookie sheet covered with parchment paper. Allow for cooling for an hour.
4. You can either serve the nuts right away or store any leftovers for up to three weeks in an airtight jar.

Nutritional Info: Calories 194; Fat 16.4g; Sodium 55mg; Carbs 10.4g; Fiber 2g; Sugar 5.6g; Protein 4g

Savory Balsamic Sausage Bites

Preparation time: 15 minutes
Cooking time: 4 to 6 hours
Serves: 18 to 20

Ingredients
- 1 medium sweet yellow onion, sliced
- 2 sweet apples, peeled, cored, sliced
- 2 pounds chicken apple sausage links, sliced into ½" rounds
- 4 tbsps spicy brown mustard
- 4 tbsps balsamic vinegar
- ⅓ cup honey

Instructions:
1. Spray nonstick cooking spray on your crock.
2. Place the sausages on top of the onions and apples in the bottom of the crock.
3. In a mixing bowl, combine the honey, balsamic vinegar, and mustard. Pour this over the food in the slow cooker.
4. Cook on low for 4-6 hours, covered. To serve, toothpicks are employed.

Nutritional Info: Calories 67; Fat 0.4g; Sodium 38mg; Carbs 16.7g; Fiber 1.6g; Sugar 14.6g; Protein 0.4g

Garlic Chicken Lettuce Wraps

Preparation time: 15 minutes
Cooking time: 2 to 3 hours
Serves: 12

Ingredients
- 2 pounds ground chicken, browned
- 4 cloves garlic, minced
- ½ cup minced sweet yellow onion
- 4 tbsps gluten-free soy sauce or Bragg's liquid aminos
- 1 tbsp natural crunchy peanut butter
- 1 teaspoon rice wine vinegar
- 1 teaspoon sesame oil
- ¼ teaspoon kosher salt
- ¼ teaspoon red pepper flakes
- ¼ teaspoon black pepper
- 1 8-ounce can sliced water chestnuts, drained, rinsed, chopped
- 3 green onions, sliced
- 12 good-sized pieces of iceberg lettuce, rinsed and patted dry

Instructions:
1. In the cooker, combine the ground chicken, garlic, yellow onion, soy sauce or liquid aminos, peanut butter, vinegar, sesame oil, salt, and black pepper.
2. Cook on low for two to three hours, covered.
3. Add the water chestnuts and green onions and cook until tender. covered, for an additional 10 to 15 minutes.
4. Generously spoon a portion of it onto each iceberg lettuce leaf.
5. Serve garnished with diced red bell pepper and green onion.

Nutritional Info: Calories 170; Fat 7.6g; Sodium 280mg; Carbs 13g; Fiber 2.6g; Sugar 1.8g; Protein 15g

Cornbread Pancakes

Preparation time: 5 minutes
Cooking time: 10 minutes
Servings: 5

Ingredients
- ¾ cup cornmeal
- ¾ cup flour, all-purpose
- 3 tbsp butter, cooled and melted
- 2 tbsp white sugar
- ½ tsp baking soda
- ½ tsp baking powder
- ½ tsp salt
- 2 eggs, large
- 1 ¼ cups of buttermilk

Instructions:
1. In a bowl, combine the cornmeal, flour, sugar, baking soda, salt, and baking powder. Add the eggs, buttermilk, and butter to a separate bowl. Blend the dry mixture with the liquid mixture until they are completely blended.
2. Heat the skillet or griddle over medium heat, lightly oiled. Add ¼ cup of batter to each cake and cook for about two minutes, or until golden. Turn off the heat for about one minute, or until brown. Repeat with the remaining battery.

Nutritional Info: Calories: 278 kcal; Fat: 10 g; Carbs: 38.9 g; Protein: 8.1 g

Creamy Seafood Dip

Preparation time: 5 to 10 minutes
Cooking time: 3 hours
Serves: 3

Ingredients
- 1 10-ounce package fat-free cream cheese
- 1 8-ounce package imitation crab strands
- 2 tbsps onion, finely chopped
- 4–5 drops hot sauce
- ¼ cup walnuts, finely chopped
- 1 teaspoon paprika

Instructions:
1. Blend all the ingredients, excluding the nuts and paprika, until well blended. 2.
2. Prepare in a slow cooker. Add some nuts and paprika.
3. Cook on low for three hours.
4. Add cilantro, parsley, and cayenne pepper as garnishes.

Nutritional Info: Calories 55; Fat 3.7g; Sodium 149mg; Carbs 1.3g; Fiber 0.1g; Sugar 0.8g; Protein 4g

Garlic Flaxseed Crackers

Preparation time: 5 minutes
Cooking time: 30 minutes
Serves: 1

Ingredients
- 1 cup ground flaxseed
- 1 teaspoon powdered garlic
- 1 teaspoon powdered onion
- 1 teaspoon cayenne pepper
- ½ cup water

Instructions:
1. Fill an appropriate mixing basin with all of the ingredients. 2.
2. Stir in the water until a dough forms.
3. Allow the dough to rest for 10 minutes.
4. Spread the dough out on a baking sheet covered with parchment paper. With the aid of a second piece of parchment paper, roll the dough into a narrow rectangle.
5. Using a sharp knife, cut into squares.
6. Place the squares on a baking sheet that has been lined with parchment paper.
7. Bake at 400°F for 30 minutes, rotating halfway through to ensure crispness on both sides.

Nutritional Info: Calories 921; Fat 71g; Sodium 57mg; Carbs 53.7g; Fiber 47g; Sugar 3g; Protein 31.7g

Nuts And Seed Bowls

Preparation time: 5 minutes
Cooking time: 20 minutes
Servings: 6

Ingredients:
- 1 cup walnuts
- 1 cup almonds
- 1 tbsp sunflower seeds
- 2 tbsps olive oil
- A pinch of salt and black pepper
- ½ tsp sweet paprika

Instructions:
1. In a dish, combine the walnuts, almonds, seeds, and other ingredients. toss, and then spread them on a baking sheet lined with parchment paper.
2. Bake for 20 minutes at 400°F, then divide and serve as a quick meal.

Nutritional Info: Calories: 150 g; Fat: 2 g; Carbs: 5 g; Protein: 5 g

Mayo Deviled Eggs with Veggies

Preparation time: 8 minutes
Cooking time: None
Serves: 8

Ingredients
- 8 hard-boiled eggs, peeled
- 4 tsp mayonnaise
- 14 cups cooked spinach
- 2 ounces chopped artichokes
- ½ teaspoon Dijon mustard
- ¼ cup grated Parmesan cheese
- ½ teaspoon powdered garlic
- 1 teaspoon salt
- ½ teaspoon black pepper

Instructions:
1. Halve hard-boiled eggs lengthwise.
2. Scoop the yolks of the eggs into a basin.
3. Combine the mayonnaise, spinach, artichokes, mustard, garlic powder, Parmesan cheese, salt, and pepper in a medium mixing bowl. Use a fork to mash until a paste forms.
4. Spoon or pipe the mixture into the cavities of the egg whites (without a nozzle, as the mixture is slightly thick).
5. Before serving, top with paprika, sumac, Parmesan cheese, or chopped herbs. (Selected by you).

Nutritional Info: Calories 228; Fat 12g; Sodium 699mg; Carbs 14.4g; Fiber 8g; Sugar 2g; Protein 19.7g

Protein Pancakes

Preparation time: 10 minutes
Cooking time: 2 minutes
Servings: 4

Ingredients
- ½ tsp baking soda
- 1 cup of whole wheat flour
- ½ tsp ground cinnamon
- 1 cup cottage cheese, low-fat
- ¼ tsp salt
- ¾ cup low-fat milk
- 2 tbsp vegetable oil
- 2 eggs

Instructions:
1. In a large bowl, combine the flour, cinnamon, salt, and baking soda.
2. Combine the cottage cheese, eggs, oil, and milk in a separate bowl. 3. Pour over the flour mixture and whisk until well combined. The batter will be thick.
3. A water drop on the top sizzles and dances on a raised platform over medium heat. You should pour ¼ cup of batter onto the grid. Cook for one to two minutes, or until the surface becomes golden brown and the bubbles explode. Cook for a minute longer on the other side or until set. Keep going with the remaining batter.

Nutritional Info: Calories: 273 kca; Fat: 11.9 g l; Carbs: 26.4 g; Protein: 16.5 g

Dijon Stuffed Eggs

Preparation time: 10 minutes
Cooking time: 10 minutes
Serves: 2

Ingredients
- Approximately 8-10 hard-boiled eggs
- 5 spears of asparagus
- 3 tsp mayonnaise
- ½ teaspoon Dijon mustard
- 2 finely chopped spring onions
- 1 teaspoon capers, chopped
- ½ teaspoon salt
- ½ teaspoon black pepper
- 1 tbsp chopped chives for garnish

Instructions:
1. Trim the asparagus stalks' crowns and remove the rough bottom ends. The tips should be set aside for decoration.
2. Half-fill a pot with water, then add the remaining stalks. Until soft, simmer for 10 minutes with a lid on after bringing to a boil.
3. Drain the asparagus stalks and slice them thinly.
4. Hard-boiled eggs: Halve them after removing the yolks and setting the whites aside. In a bowl, mix together the egg yolks, asparagus spears, mayonnaise, spring onions, capers, and mustard.
5. To taste, add salt and pepper to the food.
6. Spoon the mixture into the hard-boiled eggs using a piping bag that has been filled halfway. Or you may spoon the mixture in.
7. Slice the asparagus tip into fourths, then place it on top of the eggs.
8. Distribute the minced chives on top of the eggs.
9. Eat and enjoy yourself!

Nutritional Info: Calories 375; Fat 25g; Sodium 914mg; Carbs 5.7g; Fiber 0.9g; Sugar 3.4g; Protein 29g

Fantastic Chex Mix

Preparation time: 8 minutes
Cooking time: 1 hour
Serves: 12

Ingredients
- 3 cups gluten-free Rice Chex
- 3 cups gluten-free Corn Chex
- 3 cups gluten-free Cheerios
- 1 cup unsalted peanuts
- ⅓ cup coconut oil, melted
- 4 tsp gluten-free Worcestershire sauce
- 1 teaspoon sea salt
- 1 teaspoon garlic powder
- 1 teaspoon onion powder

Instructions:
1. Spray nonstick cooking spray on the crock.
2. Toss in the Cheerios, Rice Chex, Corn Chex, and peanuts.
3. In a small bowl, combine the Worcestershire sauce, sea salt, garlic powder, and onion powder with the coconut oil. This should be poured over the cereal in the crock and gently stirred with a rubber spatula until coated.
4. Cook on low for 3 hours, covering with a paper towel or thin dishcloth. Stir once after the first hour, twice after the second hour, and once after the third.
5. Spread the mixture out on parchment-lined baking sheets and let it cool for an hour. 6.
6. Transfer to an airtight container to serve or store.

Nutritional Info: Calories 398; Fat 20.3g; Sodium 270mg; Carbs 54.7g; Fiber 10.5g; Sugar 1.5g; Protein 11.5g

Unique Apple Butter

Preparation time: 20 minutes
Cooking time: 12 to 14 hours
Serves: 24

Ingredients
- 4 pounds apples
- 2 tsp cinnamon
- ½ teaspoon ground cloves

Instructions:
1. Apples need to be cored, peeled, and sliced. Place all the ingredients in the slow cooker.
2. Cover it with something and leave it on high for two to three hours. Turn down the heat to a low level and cook for eight hours. Apples should be half-cooked and have a deep brown hue.
3. Stir in the spices thoroughly. Cook for two to three hours on high with the cover off. Stir the ingredients thoroughly until they are smooth.
4. Either pour the mixture into sterilized jars and seal them, or transfer them to freezer containers and freeze.

Nutritional Info: Calories 38; Fat 0.1g; Sodium 1mg; Carbs 10.2g; Fiber 2g; Sugar 7.6g; Protein 0.2g

Protein Bars

Preparation time: 15 minutes
Cooking time: 15 minutes
Servings: 16

Ingredients
- ½ cup sunflower seeds
- 3 cups of rolled oats
- ½ cup shredded coconut, unsweetened
- 1 tsp ground cinnamon
- ¼ cup brown sugar
- 1 tsp sea salt
- ½ cup melted peanut butter
- 1 cup yogurt, plain Greek
- 6 tbsp pure maple syrup
- 1 tsp vanilla extract
- ¼ cup melted coconut oil
- 1 (2 oz) chopped bar dark chocolate
- 1 cup vanilla protein powder

Instructions:
1. Preheat the oven to 350°F (180°C). 2. Grease a 13-by-9-inch baking dish with cooking spray.
3. In a large mixing basin, combine the oats, coconut, sunflower seeds, cinnamon, sea salt, and brown sugar.
4. In a separate dish, combine the coconut oil, yogurt, maple syrup, vanilla extract, and peanut butter and whisk until smooth.
5. Add the oats to the mixture and put it on the grill.
6. After combining the chocolate and protein powder in a mixing bowl, distribute them onto a prepared baking tray.
7. Bake for 50 minutes in a preheated oven, or until golden brown.

Nutritional Info: Calories: 313 kcal; Fat: 16 g; Carbs: 25.5 g; Protein: 23.8 g

Enticing Turkey-Quinoa Meatballs

Preparation time: 30 minutes
Cooking time: 6 hours
Serves: 8

Ingredients
- 2 pounds lean ground turkey
- ⅔ cup cooked quinoa
- 6 cloves garlic, minced, divided
- 1 egg lightly beaten
- 2 tbsps grated Parmesan
- 3 tbsps Italian seasoning, divided
- 3 tsp onion powder, divided
- 1¾ tsp kosher salt
- 1 teaspoon pepper, divided
- 4 tbsps olive oil
- 2 28-ounce cans low-sodium crushed tomatoes
- 1 6-ounce can low-sodium tomato paste
- ¼ cup balsamic vinegar

Instructions:
1. In a mixing dish, combine the ground turkey, quinoa, egg, Parmesan cheese, 1 tbsp Italian seasoning, 1 teaspoon onion powder, 34 tsp kosher salt, and 12 tsp pepper. Make meatballs measuring 12" out of the mixture.
2. Lightly brown each meatball on all sides in a large skillet over medium-high heat by using 2 tbsps of olive oil. Take them out of the picture.
3. Mix the tomato paste, crushed tomatoes, remaining 3 minced garlic cloves, 2 tbsps Italian seasoning, 2 tsp onion powder, 1 teaspoon kosher salt, 1 teaspoon pepper, 2 tbsps olive oil, and ¼ cup balsamic vinegar in a large mixing bowl.
4. Place all of the miniature meatballs on top of half of the tomato sauce mixture in the crock. Add the last bit of tomato sauce on top to complete.
5. Covered, cook on low for 6 hours.
6. Serve with intriguing decorative toothpicks and garnish with diced fresh basil or green onion slices. 3 minuscule meatballs.

Nutritional Info: Calories 371; Fat 20g; Sodium 1042mg; Carbs 19g; Fiber 3g; Sugar 10.5g; Protein 28g

Almond 'You Must Be

Preparation time: 15 minutes
Cooking time: 15 minutes
Servings: 5

Ingredients:
- 2 tbsp finely chopped walnuts
- 1 ½ tsp olive oil
- 1 cup of almond flour
- 1 ½ tsp flaxseed meal
- 2 tbsp Water
- ½ tsp salt

Instructions:
1. Preheat the oven to 350° F.Lining the baking sheet with parchment paper
2. In a mixing dish, combine the nuts, almond flour, salt, and flaxseed meal. Olive oil and water should be combined until the dough becomes sticky and adheres together.
3. Spread the dough out on the prepared baking sheet. Give the dough a second layer of pastry. Use a rolling pin to stretch the dough into a rectangle that is 1/16 of an inch wide. Remove the top portion of the church bread, then shape the dough into a rectangle by cutting the edges. Re-roll the leftover dough until it is a uniform thickness in the corners or at one end of the rectangle.
4. Holding the dough attached, cut it into 1-inch squares using a pizza cutter.
5. Bake for fifty minutes in a preheated oven or until the dough's outside edges are golden. Before cutting the crackers into squares, allow them to cool on a baking sheet.
6. If necessary, replace the one cup of almond flour with a mixture of ⅔ cup almond meal and ⅓ cup pumpkin seed flour.

Nutritional Info: Calories: 36 kcal; Fat: 3.7 g; Carbs: 0.6 g; Protein: 0.6 g

Hummus With Ground Lamb

Preparation time: 10 minutes
Cooking time: 15 minutes
Servings: 8

Ingredients
- 10 ounces hummus
- 12 ounces lamb meat, ground
- ½ cup pomegranate seeds
- ¼ cup parsley, chopped
- 1 tbsp olive oil
- Pita chips for serving

Instructions:
1. Brown the meat for about 15 minutes over medium heat in a pan, turning often.
2. Spread hummus on a plate, top with ground lamb, garnish with parsley, and serve with pita chips as an appetizer.

Nutritional Info: Calories: 133 kcal; Fat: 9.7 g; Carbs: 6.4 g; Protein: 5.4 g

Zucchini Protein Pancakes

Preparation time: 10 minutes
Cooking time: 5 minutes
Servings: 1

Ingredients
- 1 small shredded zucchini
- ½ cup oats, old-fashioned
- 1 egg
- 1 scoop of protein powder
- 2 tbsp coconut flour
- cooking spray
- 1 tbsp stevia powder

Instructions:
1. Place the oats in a blender and pulse them three to four times to make them grainy. After that, transfer the oatmeal to a bowl.
2. Make a batter with the oats, egg, zucchini, coconut flour, spinach, and protein powder.
3. Heat a pan and spray it with cooking spray. Leak the battery into the pan. About three minutes of cooking time or until the edges become dry. Cook for another two minutes after turning.

Nutritional Info: Calories: 364 kcal; Fat: 9.1 g; Carbs: 48.3 g; Protein: 28.8 g

Stuffed Avocado

Preparation time: 10 minutes
Cooking time: 0 minutes
Servings: 2

Ingredients
- 1 avocado, halved and pitted
- 10 ounces canned tuna, drained
- 2 tbsps sun-dried tomatoes, chopped
- 1 and ½ tbsp basil pesto
- 2 tbsps black olives, pitted and chopped
- Salt and black pepper to the taste
- 2 tsps pine nuts, toasted and chopped
- 1 tbsp basil, chopped

Instructions:
1. Combine the tuna, sun-dried tomatoes, and the other ingredients (aside from the avocado) in a bowl.
2. Stuff the avocado halves with the tuna mixture as an appetizer.

Nutritional Info: Calories: 233 kcal; Fat: 9 g; Carbs: 11.4 g; Protein: 5.6 g

Salad On A Stick

Preparation time: 15 minutes
Cooking time: 0 minutes
Servings: 8

Ingredients
- 8 (½ inch) cubes of feta cheese
- 2 tbsp dried oregano
- 8 bamboo toothpick
- 8 grape tomatoes
- 8 ½-inch slices of cucumber
- 8 pitted Kalamata olives

Instructions:
1. Place some oregano in a basin. Roll each of the feta cheese cubes in order to coat them after that.
2. Thread a toothpick with one cucumber, one tomato, one lettuce cube, and one olive. Use the remaining toothpicks to continue.

Nutritional Info: Calories: 53 kcal; Fat: 3.7 g; Carbs: 3.1 g; Protein: 2.4 g

Sesame Seed Balls

Preparation time: 20 minutes
Cooking time: 5 minutes
Servings: 12

Ingredients
- ¼ cup of oats
- 1 cup of whole wheat flour
- 3 tbsp ground flax seed
- ¼ tsp salt
- ½ tsp ground cinnamon
- ½ cup of sesame seeds
- ½ cup of honey
- ⅔ cup of crunchy peanut butter

Instructions:
1. Add the blueberries and strawberries to a bowl. Sprinkle the sugar on top and combine to coat the berries.
2. Put two parfait glasses at the bottom with 2 tbsp of granola. Add 2 tbsps of yogurt and sprinkle on ½ teaspoon of lemon zest. Top with ⅓ of the berries. Continue adding layers until the parfait glasses are filled.

Nutritional Info: Calories: 264 kcal; Fat: 14.1 g; Carbs: 26.2 g; Protein: 9 g

White Bean Dip

Preparation time: 10 minutes
Cooking time: 0 minutes
Servings: 4

Ingredients
- Zest of ¼ lemon
- 2 tbsps olive oil
- 15 ounces canned beans, drained and rinsed
- 5-6 canned artichoke hearts, drained and quartered
- 3 garlic cloves, minced
- 1 tbsp basil, chopped
- Juice of ¼ lemon
- Salt & black pepper to taste

Instructions:
1. Combine the beans, artichokes, and the other ingredients in a food processor, leaving out the oil.
2. Gradually add the oil. Give the mixture one more quick pulse. Divide it among glasses and serve as a party dip.

Nutritional Info: Calories: 27 kcal; Fat: 11.7 g; Carbs: 18.5 g; Protein: 16.5 g

Eggplant Dip

Preparation time: 10 minutes
Cooking time: 40 minutes
Servings: 4

Ingredients
- 1 eggplant, poked with a fork
- 2 tbsps tahini paste
- 1 tbsp parsley, chopped
- tbsps lemon juice
- 2 tbsp olive oil
- 3 garlic cloves, crushed
- Salt and black pepper to taste

Instructions:
1. Place the eggplant in a roasting pan, bake it at 400 degrees Fahrenheit for 40 minutes, let it cool, peel it, and then transfer it to your food processor. 2.
2. Mix in the remaining ingredients, excluding the parsley, until well combined. Divide the mixture into small dishes and serve as an appetizer with the parsley sprinkled on top.

Nutritional Info: Calories: 121 kcal; Fat: 4.3 g; Carbs: 1.4 g; Protein: 4.3 g

Lemony Artichokes

Preparation time: 20 minutes
Cooking time: 2 to 10 hours
Serves: 4

Ingredients
- 4 artichokes
- 1 teaspoon salt
- 2 tbsps lemon juice

Instructions:
1. Artichokes should be washed and trimmed, with the tops being taken off and the stems being cut flush with the bottoms. Stand straight inside the slow cooker.
2. In a basin, mix the salt and lemon juice. Pour the mixture over the artichokes.
3. Pour water onto the dish until 34% of the artichokes are submerged.
4. Cover. 2-4 hours on high or 8-10 hours on low.
5. Spoon some of the melted butter on top before serving.

Nutritional Info: Calories 62; Fat 0.2g; Sodium 702mg; Carbs 14g; Fiber 7g; Sugar 1.5g; Protein 4g

Date Balls

Preparation time: 10 minutes
Cooking time: 30 minutes
Servings: 20–24

Ingredients
- 1 cup of pitted Dates
- 1 cup of shredded Soft-Jelly Coconut
- ½ cup of Sesame Seeds
- ½ cup of Brazil Nuts*
- ¼ cup of Agave Syrup
- ½ tsp. of Pure Sea Salt

Instructions:
1. In a food processor or blender, combine dates, shredded coconut, Brazil nuts*, agave syrup, and pure sea salt. It should be blended well for 20 to 30 seconds.
2. Form a ball with a spoonful of the prepared mixture in your hand.
3. Place the same seeds in a sizable bowl and roll the date balls in the mixture.
4. Repeat steps 3 and 4 until all of the date mixture has been consumed.

Nutritional Info: Calories: 152 kcal; Fat: 0 g; Carbs: 6 g; Protein: 20g

Veggie Fritters

Preparation time: 10 minutes
Cooking time: 10 minutes
Servings: 8

Ingredients
- 3 garlic cloves, minced
- 2 yellow onions, chopped
- 2 scallions, chopped
- 2 carrots, grated
- 2 tsps cumin, ground
- ½ tsp turmeric powder
- Salt and black pepper to the taste
- ¼ tsp coriander, ground
- 1 tbsps parsley, chopped
- ¼ tsp lemon juice
- ½ cup almond flour
- 2 beets, peeled and grated
- 2 eggs, whisked
- ¼ cup tapioca flour
- 2 tbsps olive oil

Instructions:
1. Add the garlic to a bowl along with the onions, scallions, and the other ingredients (but not the oil), and whisk to thoroughly blend.
2. Heat the pan over medium-high heat. Add the fries. Cook for 5 minutes.

Nutritional Info: Calories: 209 kcal; Fat: 11.2 g; Carbs: 4.4 g; Protein: 4.8 g

Protein-Rich Vegan Pancakes

Preparation time: 10 minutes
Cooking time: 25 minutes
Servings: 6

Ingredients
- 4 tbsp egg replacer, dry vegan
- 1 cup of ice-cold water
- 1 cup of all-purpose flour
- 4 tbsp flaxseed meal
- 1 cup almond flour, blanched
- 2 tbsp white sugar
- 1 tsp baking soda
- 2 tsp baking powder
- 2 cups of almond milk
- 2 tsp vanilla extract
- 5 tbsp vegan butter

Instructions:
1. In a large mixing bowl, combine vegan egg replacer and ice-cold water with an electric mixer until thick.
2. In the second dish, combine the all-purpose flour, flaxseed meal, baking powder, baking soda, and sugar and whisk until smooth. In a third dish, combine almond milk, vanilla extract, and four tbsps of vegan butter.
3. Alternately add the flour mixture and almond milk mixture to the mixture of vegetarian eggs using a blender set to medium speed.
4. In a large pan over medium heat, melt one tbsp of vegetable butter. Pour half a cup of cake batter into the pan and cook for two to three minutes, or until bubbles start to form on the top. Cook the sides for a further two minutes, or until light brown. Continue with the remaining batter, adding more vegetable butter as necessary.

Nutritional Info: Calories: 368 kcal; Fat: 22.5 g; Carbs: 34.6 g; Protein: 7.8 g

Olive Tapenade With Anchovies

Preparation time: 1hour and 10 minutes
Cooking time: 0 minutes
Servings: 2

Ingredients
- 2 cups pitted Kalamata olives or other black olives
- 2 Anchovy fillets, chopped
- 2 tsps chopped capers
- 1 garlic clove, finely minced
- 1 cooked egg yolk
- 1 tsp Dijon mustard
- ¼ cup extra-virgin olive oil
- Seedy Crackers, Versatile Sandwich Round, or vegetables for serving (optional)

Instructions:
1. Rinse the olives in cold water, then dry them well. Place the drained olives, anchovies, capers, garlic, egg yolk, and Dijon in a food processor, blender, or large jar (if using an immersion blender).
2. Continue until a thick paste develops. Gradually splash in the olive oil as you run. Pour into a small bowl, cover, and place in the refrigerator for at least an hour to allow the flavors to meld.
3. Serve with crunchy vegetables of your choice or on top of a vegetarian sandwich round.

Nutritional Info: Calories: 179 kcal; Fat: 19 g; Carbs: 2 g; Protein: 2 g

Smoked Salmon Crudités

Preparation time: 10 minutes
Cooking time: 15 minutes
Servings: 4

Ingredients
- 4 ounces smoked wild salmon
- 2 tbsps Roasted Garlic Aioli
- 1 tbsp Dijon mustard
- 1 tbsp chopped scallions, green parts only
- 2 tsps chopped capers
- ½ tsp dried dill
- Pinch endive spears or hearts of romaine
- ½ English cucumber, cut into ¼-inch-thick rounds

Instructions:
1. Cut the smoked salmon roughly and place it in a small bowl.2. Add the aioli, Dijon, scallops, capers, and dill, then combine well.
2. Serve chilled, with a dollop of the smoked salmon mixture on top of the cucumber rounds and endivve spreads.

Nutritional Info: Calories: 92 kcal; Fat: 5 g; Carbs: 1 g; Protein: 9 g

Marinated Feta And Artichokes

Preparation time: 10 minutes, plus 4 hours of inactive time
Cooking time: 10 minutes
Servings: 2

Ingredients
- 4 ounces traditional Greek feta, cut into ½-inch cubes
- 4 ounces drained artichoke hearts, quartered lengthwise
- ⅓ cup extra-virgin olive oil
- Zest and juice of 1 lemon
- 2 tbsps roughly chopped fresh rosemary
- 2 tbsps roughly chopped fresh parsley
- ½ tsp black peppercorns

Instructions:
1. Combine the feta and artichoke hearts in a glass bowl.2. Add the olive oil, lemon zest and juice, rosemary, parsley, and peppercorns; toss well to coat, being careful not to break up the quinoa.
2. Allow to cool for up to 4 days or 4 hours. Take the food out of the fridge 30 minutes before serving.

Nutritional Info: Calories: 235 kcal; Fat: 23 g; Carbs: 1 g; Protein: 4 g

Citrus-Marinated Olives

Preparation time: 4 hours
Cooking time: 0 minutes
Servings: 2

Ingredients
- 2 Cups mixed green olives with pits
- ¼ cup red wine vinegar
- ¼ cup extra-virgin olive oil
- 3 Garlic cloves, finely minced
- Zest and juice of 1 large orange
- 1 tsp red pepper flakes
- ¼ cup Bay leaves
- ½ tsp ground cumin
- ½ tsp ground allspice

Instructions:
1. Combine the oil, vinegar, garlic, orange zest and juice, red pepper flakes, bay leaves, cumin, and allspice.
2. Cover and chill for up to a week to allow the olives to marinate, then mix again before serving.

Nutritional Info: Calories: 133 kcal; Fat: 14 g; Carbs: 2 g; Protein: 1 g

Boiled Unshelled Peanuts

Preparation time: 5 minutes
Cooking time: 7 to 8 hours
Serves: 32

Ingredients
- 2 pounds raw peanuts in the shell
- 7 tbsps salt water to cover peanuts

Instructions:
1. Rinse unshelled peanuts thoroughly in cold water.
2. In your slow cooker crock, soak the peanuts overnight in water with 7 tbsps of salt.
3. In the morning, reduce the heat to low and cook the peanuts for 7 to 10 hours, or until they are soft. Boiling peanuts should have soft, pliable shells rather than crispy, rigid ones.
4. After draining the peanuts, let them cool for ten minutes before serving. Eat the peanuts after removing their shells.
5. Keep any leftover boiled peanuts in the refrigerator or freezer. Reheat the meal before serving.

Nutritional Info: Calories 160; Fat 13.8g; Sodium 3mg; Carbs 4.7g; Fiber 2.4g; Sugar 1g; Protein 7g

Tuna Croquettes

Preparation time: 40 minutes
Cooking time: 25 minutes
Servings: 36

Ingredients
- 2 tbsps extra-virgin olive oil, plus 1 to 2 cups
- 2 tbsps almond flour, plus 1 cup, divided
- 1 ¼ cups heavy cream
- 1 (4-ounce) can olive oil-packed yellowfin tuna
- 1 tbsp chopped red onion
- 2 tsps minced capers
- ½ tsp dried dill
- ¼ tsp freshly ground black pepper
- 5 large eggs
- 1 cup panko breadcrumbs (or a gluten-free version)

Instructions:
1. Warm up 6 tbsps of olive oil in a large skillet over medium-low heat.2. Add 5 tbsps of almond flour, and simmer while constantly stirring for 2 to 3 minutes, or until a smooth paste develops and the flour begins to color.
2. Increase the heat to medium-high and whisk in the heavy cream gradually.Continue whisking for an additional 4 to 5 minutes, or until the mixture is completely smooth and thick. Remove and add the tuna, chopped capsicum, dill, and pepper.
3. Pour the mixture into an 8-inch square baking dish that has been well coated in olive oil and set outside at room temperature.
4. Wrap in plastic wrap and set aside for four hours or overnight.Set up three bowls to create the croquette shapes. Beat the eggs together in one.
5. Stir in the remaining almond flour.In the third step, add the panko.Set a baking sheet on parchment paper.
6. Scoop about a tbsp of the chilled, prepared dough into the flour mixture and roll to coat. Shake off the excess and roll into an oval with your hands.
7. Dip the croquette into the cooked egg before gently coating it with panko. Place on a lined baking sheet, then repeat with the leftover dough.
8. Warm up the remaining 1 to 2 cups of olive oil over medium-high heat in a small sauté pan.
9. Once the oil is hot, cook the croquettes three or four at a time, depending on the size of your pan, and remove them with a slotted spoon once they are golden brown.
10. To prevent burning, you will sometimes need to adjust the oil temperature. Lower the temperature if the croquet greens soon become a dark brown color.

Nutritional Info: Calories: 245 kcal; Fat: 22 g; Carbs: 1 g; Protein: 6 g

Desserts

Chocolate Protein Muffins

Preparation time: 10 minutes
Cooking time: 20 minutes
Servings: 9

Ingredients
- ¾ cup flour, all-purpose
- 2 packets of Chocolate Protein Powder
- ½ tsp baking soda
- ¼ tsp salt
- ½ tsp baking powder
- ½ cup applesauce
- ⅓ cup white sugar
- ½ cup plain Greek yogurt, low-fat
- 1 egg
- ½ cup of dark chocolate chips
- ¾ tsp vanilla extract

Instructions:
1. 400 degrees Fahrenheit or lessWarm up your ovaries first.Place the nine muffins on a baking sheet or nonstick surface.
2. In a bowl, combine the flour, powdered drink mix, baking soda, salt, and baking powder. 3.
3. In a separate dish, combine the yogurt, apricot preserve, sugar, vanilla extract, and egg. Add the flour mixture and toss well before adding the chocolate chips.
4.Bake for seven minutes in the oven, then reduce the temperature to 350 degrees Fahrenheit.
5. Bake the muffins for ten to twenty minutes, or until they bounce back when touched.

Nutritional Info: Calories: 170 kcal; Fat: 4.4 g; Carbs: 29.9 g; Protein: 4.1 g

Protein Pumpkin Muffins

Preparation time: 5 minutes
Cooking time: 17 minutes
Servings: 24

Ingredients
- 1 ½ cups flour, all-purpose
- 2 cups protein supplement, powdered
- 1 ½ tsp salt
- 2 tsp ground cinnamon
- 2 tsp ground nutmeg
- 1 cup white sugar
- 1 ½ cups applesauce
- 1 cup vegetable oil
- 2 eggs
- 1 (15 oz) can of pumpkin puree, canned
- 2 egg whites
- 1 cup walnuts, chopped
- ½ cup water

Instructions:
1. Preheat the oven to 350 degrees Fahrenheit.Use muffin liners to grease the muffin cups.
2. In a bowl, combine the flour, protein powder, salt, cinnamon, sugar, and nutmeg. Add the sugar, oil, eggs, pumpkin, water, and egg whites and combine everything well.
3. Stir the nuts into the batter before spooning it into the muffin tins.
4. Bake the muffins in the oven for 60 minutes, or until a toothpick inserted into the middle of the muffin comes out clean.

Nutritional Info: Calories: 246 kcal; Fat: 13.4 g; Carbs: 22.2 g; Protein: 10 g

Protein Bites

Preparation time: 20 minutes
Cooking time: 1 hour
Servings: 48

Ingredients
- ⅔ cup of soy protein powder
- 2 cups flour, all-purpose
- ⅓ cup of oat flour
- 1 cup brown sugar
- 1 cup white sugar
- ½ cup yogurt, plain Greek
- 2 tsp vanilla extract
- ½ cup softened butter
- 2 cups of chocolate chips
- 2 tbsp milk

Instructions:
1. In a mixing bowl, combine all-purpose flour, oat flour, and soy protein powder.
2. In a large mixing bowl, combine the yogurt, brown sugar, white sugar, butter, and salt with an electric mixer until smooth and creamy.3. Pour the vanilla extract in. Add the flour mixture back in. One tbsp of milk at a time, until the batter is smooth and thick. Chocolate pieces need to be folded in.
3. Roll the battery into 1-inch balls with your hands.
4. Set it on a baking pan. Move to the freezer and chill for an hour, or chill in the refrigerator for two to three hours.

Nutritional Info: Calories: 118 kcal; Fat: 4.4 g; Carbs: 18.3 g; Protein: 2.3 g

Protein Truffles

Preparation time: 10 minutes
Cooking time: 0 minutes
Servings: 20

Ingredients
- ½ cup honey peanut butter, roasted
- ½ cup ricotta cheese, whole-milk
- ⅓ cup dry roasted peanuts, chopped
- 2 tbsp peanut butter-flavored syrup, sugar-free
- 2 scoops of vanilla protein powder
- 1 tsp vanilla extract
- 1 pinch of salt
- 2 packets of stevia-erythritol sweetener

Instructions:
1. In a bowl, combine the ricotta cheese, vanilla extract, and maple syrup. Use a hand mixer to thoroughly stir it. Blend in the sweetener, salt, and protein powder until smooth.
2. Shape the mixture into one-inch balls. Coat in peanut butter.
3. Refrigerate until ready to serve.

Nutritional Info: Calories: 70 kcal; Fat: 4.6 g; Carbs: 2.3 g; Protein: 5.9 g

Banana Pie

Preparation time: 15 minutes
Cooking time: 40 minutes plus 4 hours chilling
Servings: 6–8

Ingredients
Crust
- 1-½ cups of pitted Dates
- 1-½ cups of shredded Soft-Jelly Coconut
- ¼ cup of Agave Syrup
- ¼ tsp. of Pure Sea Salt

Filling
- 6–8 Burro Bananas
- 1 cup of Homemade Hempseed Milk
- 7 ounces of Organic Creamed Unsweetened Coconut
- 4 tbsp. of Agave Syrup
- ⅛ tsp. of Pure Sea Salt

Instructions:
1. Blend the ingredients for the crust in a blender for about 30 seconds, or until a ball forms.
2. Press the crust mixture into a circular pie pan and top with pastry puff. Store it for 10 minutes in the refrigerator.
3. Combine all of the ingredients for the filling in a large bowl.
4. After pouring the filling into a pan, shake the sides to spread it out.
5. To firm up the pie, cover it with foil and place it in the freezer for about 4 hours.

Nutritional Info: Calories: 105 kcal; Fat: 0 g; Carbs: 8 g; Protein: 27 g

"Chocolate" Pudding

Preparation time: 10 minutes
Cooking time: 20 minutes
Servings: 4

Ingredients
- 1 to 2 cups of Black Sapote
- ¼ cup of Agave Syrup
- ½ cup of soaked Brazil Nuts (overnight or for at least 3 hours)
- 1 tbsp. of Hemp Seeds
- ½ cup of Water

Instructions:
1. Halve one to two cups of black preserves. Remove all of the grass.
2. Consume a full cup of peeled fruit.
3. In a blender, combine all of the ingredients and blend until smooth.
4. Serve and enjoy your pudding, "chocolate"!

Nutritional Info: Calories: 87 kcal; Fat: 3 g; Carbs: 12 g; Protein: 3 g

Vegan Mango Ice Cream with Brazil Nuts

Preparation time: 5 minutes
Cooking time: 20 minutes
Servings: 1

Ingredients
- 4 ripe peeled mangoes, chopped
- ¾ cups of coconut milk
- 3-4 tbsp crushed Brazil nuts

Instructions:
1. Get your icing cream maker ready. Blend the mangoes until they are smooth, then pour the puree into the bowl of the ice cream maker. Pour milk into the dish containing the mangoes after processing them in a blender a few times.
2. Start the ice cream maker for about 10 minutes, or until it begins to thicken. Add some Brazil nuts while saving a few for garnish. Scoop the icing cream into a container, then place it in the freezer for a few hours to set.
3. Sprinkle with roasted Brazil nuts and serve.

Nutritional Info: Calories: 141 kcal; Fat: 2.7g; Carbs: 18 g; Protein: 22.7 g

Strawberry-Applesauce Nice Cream

Preparation time: 10 minutes
Cooking time: 8 hours
Servings: 4

Ingredients
- 3 cups of homemade applesauce
- 1 cup strawberries, frozen
- ¼ cup sea moss gel
- 3 tbsp agave nectar
- 2 tbsp homemade hemp sea moss milk
- ½ small squeezed key lime

Instructions:
1. In a blender, combine all of the ingredients and blend until thick and smooth. Adapt the flavor to work best for you.
2. Combine in a glass container and smooth out.
3. To firm up, serve soft or freeze for 2-4 hours, covered.
4. Thaw for 2 to 5 minutes before serving. The ice cream may be kept in a freezer for about two weeks.
5. Enjoy!

Nutritional Info: Calories: 196 kcal; Fat: 1 g; Carbs: 12 g; Protein: 2 g

Almond Paleo Date Cookies

Preparation time: 25 minutes
Cooking time: 15 minutes
Servings: 24

Ingredients
- 1 cup dates, chopped and pitted
- 1 tbsp vanilla extract
- 2 ½ cups of almond flour, blanched
- ½ cup cherries, chopped and dried
- 2 tbsp chia seeds
- ½ cup walnuts, chopped
- ½ cup of coconut oil
- ½ tsp of sea salt
- ½ tsp baking soda
- 1 egg
- 2 tbsp of maple syrup

Instructions:
1. Heat your oven to 400 degrees Fahrenheit. Set two baking pans in a row using parchment paper.
2. In a large mixing basin, combine the dates, almond flour, raisins, chia seeds, sea salt, walnuts, and baking soda. Using a fork or spoon, combine the egg, coconut oil, vanilla extract, and maple syrup until a dough forms.
3. Spoon the dough onto the baking sheets using a little spoon.
4. Bake for 50 minutes in a preheated oven, or until the edges start to turn golden. Turn off the oven and leave the cook inside with the door closed for a further ten minutes. Remove from the oven and set aside to cool.

Nutritional Info: Calories: 174 kcal; Fat: 13 g; Carbs: 12.3 g; Protein: 3.8 g

Blackberry Jam

Preparation time: 5 minutes
Cooking time: 12 minutes
Servings: 32

Ingredients
- 3, 6-oz, package fresh berries, rinsed
- 3 tbsp agave nectar
- 1 tbsp key lime, squeezed juice
- ¼ cup + 2 tbsp Sea moss gel

Instructions:
1. Heat the berries in a medium-sized saucepan over medium-high heat, stirring constantly, until the liquid begins to release and the berries begin to break down.
2. Stir in all of the other ingredients for about 1 minute over low heat, or until the mixture begins to thicken. Remove from the oven and set aside for about 15 minutes to cool.
3. You can store it for around 5-7 days in a refrigerator or for roughly 2 months in a freezer.
4. Serve with bread, cakes, or toast.

Nutritional Info: Calories: 60 kcal; Fat: 1 g; Carbs: 12 g Protein: 1 g

Wrapped Plums

Preparation time: 5 minutes
Cooking time: 0 minutes
Servings: 8

Ingredients
- 2 ounces prosciutto, cut into 16 pieces
- 1 tbsp chives, chopped
- A pinch of red pepper flakes, crushed
- 3 Plums, quartered

Instructions:
1. To serve, wrap each plum quarter in a slice of prosciutto, place on a plate, and sprinkle with chive and red pepper flakes.

Nutritional Info: Calories: 30 kcal; Fat: 1 g; Carbs: 4 g; Protein: 2 g

Homemade Whipped Cream

Preparation time: 10 minutes
Cooking time: 10 minutes
Servings: 1 cup

Ingredients
- 1 cup of Aquafaba
- ¼ cup of Agave Syrup

Instructions:
1. Pour the maple syrup and quafa into a basin.
2. Mix at high speed for 10 to 15 minutes with a hand mixer or 5 to 10 minutes with a stand mixer.
3. Enjoy your own whip cream as a snack!

Nutritional Info: Calories: 85 kcal; Fat: 2 g; Carbs: 14 g; Protein: 3 g

Chocolate Chip Oatmeal Protein Cookies

Preparation time: 15 minutes
Cooking time: 10 minutes
Servings: 23

Ingredients
- ½ cup of milk chocolate chips
- 2 cups of quick-cooking oats
- ½ cup white sugar
- 1 tsp baking soda
- 2 scoops of vanilla protein powder
- ¼ tsp salt
- 2 large eggs
- 6 tbsp smooth peanut butter
- 1 tsp vanilla extract

Instructions:
1. Set the oven's temperature to 350°F.
2. In a medium mixing bowl, combine the chocolate chips, oats, sugar, baking soda, salt, and protein powder. In a mixing dish, combine one egg, vanilla extract, and butter made from pecans. Incorporate the last egg.
3. Knead the dough until it is thick and sticky.
4. Scoop two-inch portions of dough, using a tbsp, onto baking sheets lined with parchment paper. With your hand, gently fry the cookware.
5. Bake for 10 minutes, or until the bottoms and edges are golden brown, in a preheated oven.
6. Cool for two minutes on the pan before transferring to a wire rack to cool completely.

Nutritional Info: Calories: 110 kcal; Fat: 4.4 g; Carbs: 12.5 g; Protein: 6 g

Mile-High Apple Pie

Preparation time: 25 minutes
Cooking time: 1 hour
Servings: 12

Ingredients
- 1 tbsp fresh lemon juice
- 8 Golden Delicious apples, large, cored, peeled, diced into ⅛ inch slices
- 3 tbsp potato starch
- 1 tsp ground cinnamon
- ¾ cup of white sugar
- ¼ tsp grated nutmeg, fresh
- 1 recipe pastry (for ten-inch double crust pie)
- ¼ cup unsalted butter, cold and diced into ¼-inch pieces
- 1 tbsp white sugar
- 2 tsp milk

Instructions:
1. Preheat the oven to 425 degrees F.
2. In the lowest part of the oven, place a baking stone on top of the oven rack.
3. In a large mixing bowl, combine the lemon juice and all of the ingredients.
4. In a mixing bowl, combine the ¾ cup of sugar, potato starch, nutmeg, and cinnamon.
5. Fit a ten-inch pie pan with half of the pie crust dough that has been rolled out and gently dusted with flour. Both half of the toppings and half of the butter pieces should be piled on the crust. Sprinkle ½ of the potato starch mixture over the appliances.
6. Fill the pie pan with the remaining ingredients. Sprinkle the remaining sweet mixture and buttery crumbs on top. Roll out the remaining pie crust dough and carefully place it over the aprons.
7. Crimp the edges to seal the crusts.8. Make a few holes with a fork in the outside crust. One tbsp of sugar was brushed on top of the crust.
8. In the preheated oven, put the pie on the baking stone. Reduce the temperature immediately to 350° F. Bake for approximately 60 minutes, or until the crust is golden brown. Halfway through the baking time, check the edges for over-browning and, if necessary, wrap them in aluminum foil for the last thirty minutes of baking. Allow the food to cool for three hours on a wire rack before serving.

Nutritional Info: Calories: 307 kcal; Fat: 13.8 g; Carbs: 46.6 g; Protein: 2.3 g

Conclusion

Our bodies change as we age, and we must modify our eating habits to keep up. The Whole Body Reset is the only program created specifically for people in their forties and fifties who want to maintain their lean, active, and vitality for the rest of their life.

Appendix Measurement Conversion Chart

VOLUME EQUIVALENTS (DRY)

US STANDARD	METRIC (APPROXIMATE)
⅛ teaspoon	0.5 mL
¼ teaspoon	1 mL
½ teaspoon	2 mL
¾ teaspoon	4 mL
1 teaspoon	5 mL
1 tablespoon	15 mL
¼ cup	59 mL
½ cup	118 mL
¾ cup	177 mL
1 cup	235 mL
2 cups	475 mL
3 cups	700 mL
4 cups	1 L

VOLUME EQUIVALENTS (LIQUID)

US STANDARD	US STANDARD (OUNCES)	METRIC (APPROXIMATE)
2 tablespoons	1 fl.oz	30 mL
¼ cup	2 fl.oz	60 mL
½ cup	4 fl.oz	120 mL
1 cup	8 fl.oz	240 mL
1½ cup	12 fl.oz	355 mL
2 cups or 1 pint	16 fl.oz	475 mL
4 cups or 1 quart	32 fl.oz	1 L
1 gallon	128 fl.oz	4 L

TEMPERATURES EQUIVALENTS

FAHRENHEIT (F)	CELSIUS (C) (APPROXIMATE)
225°F	107°C
250°F	120°C
275°F	135°C
300°F	150°C
325°F	160°C
350°F	180°C
375°F	190°C
400°F	205°C
425°F	220°C
450°F	235°C
475°F	245°C
500°F	260°C

WEIGHT EQUIVALENTS

US STANDARD	METRIC (APPROXINATE)
1 ounce	28 g
2 ounces	57 g
5 ounces	142 g
10 ounces	284 g
15 ounces	425 g
16 ounces (1 pound)	455 g
1.5 pounds	680 g
2 pounds	907 g

www.ingramcontent.com/pod-product-compliance
Lightning Source LLC
Chambersburg PA
CBHW081623100526
44590CB00021B/3571